An Official Whitman® Guidebook

D1125134

Adventure
Across the
States

Collecting State Quarters
and Other Coins

Whitman Publishing, LLC
Atlanta, Georgia

© 2006 Whitman Publishing, LLC
3101 Clairmont Road · Suite C · Atlanta GA 30329

Correspondence concerning this book may be directed to the publisher, at the address above.

ISBN: 0-7948-2050-6

Some images and text are used, with permission, from *A Guide Book of United States Coins* (edited by Kenneth Bressett); the *Guide Book of Modern United States Proof Coin Sets* (by David W. Lange); *History of the United States Mint and Its Coinage* (by David W. Lange); *Money of the Bible* (by Kenneth Bressett); the *Official ANA Grading Standards for United States Coins*; and *The Whitman Insider Guide to Grading United States Coins*.

Disclaimer: Expert opinion should be sought in any significant numismatic purchase. This book is presented as a guide only. No warranty or representation of any kind is made concerning the completeness or accuracy of the information presented.

For a complete catalog of numismatic reference books, supplies, and storage products, visit Whitman Publishing online at www.whitmanbooks.com.

CONTENTS

A t the age of 10, I began a journey that continues to enrich my life today. Around 1973 a close family friend gave me a Lincoln cent album for coins dated 1941 to 1971. Each week a quick trip to the bank with my allowance would produce 200 fresh cents to search for dates I needed for my budding collection. The memories are still fresh in my mind of the excitement of completing this set. It remains one of my most prized possessions.

From this small start, my career in numismatics began. Over the last 30 years, I have bought and sold millions of dollars worth of rare coins. It all began with a simple collection of Lincoln cents.

Coin collecting captures the imagination on many levels. There are the connections with historical events, monetary history, politics, and art. Who could hold a 100-year-old Morgan silver dollar and not wonder about the previous owners or what the coin might have purchased when it was issued? Ancient Roman coins that might have paid the wages of an imperial soldier can be had for just a few dollars. Very few collecting endeavors allow one to connect with the past as well as rare coins.

Today's young collectors are very fortunate because the United States Mint has recently produced many interesting and collectible coins that can still be found in circulation. The 50 State Quarters® program that began in 1999 has created many interesting and challenging issues. Most can be found with a little patience and a small budget. There are also a few rarities in the state quarter program which have been discovered that are quite valuable. The Wisconsin quarter with an extra leaf is such an example.

I strongly urge young people to give coin collecting a chance. There are many demands in today's society for young individuals, such as after-school activities, music, video games, and television. Coin collecting, on the other hand, is a hobby that can be enjoyed for a lifetime. I personally have none of the books, games, or other items of my youth, but I will enjoy my Lincoln cent collection for the rest of my life!

Jeff Garrett
President
Mid-American Rare Coin Galleries, Inc.

ACKNOWLEDGEMENTS

The publisher thanks Jeff Garrett for writing the foreword above as a welcome to this book; and also Amanda McDaniel, Tyler McDaniel, and William Pirtle, who are pictured in various photographs. Some images and text in *Adventure Across the States* are used, with permission, from *A Guide Book of United States Coins* (edited by Kenneth Bressett); the *Guide Book of Modern United States Proof Coin Sets* (by David W. Lange); *History of the United States Mint and Its Coinage* (by David W. Lange); *Money of the Bible* (by Kenneth Bressett); the *Official ANA Grading Standards for United States Coins*; and *The Whitman Insider Guide to Grading United States Coins*. Images of coin folders, albums, and other collecting supplies are used courtesy of Whitman Publishing and H.E. Harris & Co.

*H*ow do you pay for things you buy at the store? You probably use dollar bills. Grownups with bank accounts can write a check, or pay with a plastic debit card. In this book, we look at another kind of money, one that people like to *collect* as well as *spend*: coins!

People have been spending coins for almost 3,000 years. Before coins, other valuable items that people used for money included:

    cattle
    bars of salt
    elephant tails
    wampum

People would also *barter*, or trade, their goods and services. A farmer who grew vegetables, but had no milk, might barter some of his corn for a neighbor's goat. But bartering is not perfect system. I might want some corn, but if the farmer only wants milk, and I don't have a goat, how can I trade with him? Or, what if I have a goat, but the farmer lives a hundred miles away, and I can't get the goat to walk that far?

Did You Know?

Wampum is an Algonquin word that means "white shell beads." Native Americans used seashells to make little beads, and strung them together as necklaces, belts, or long strands. These beads were valuable because they were rare and beautiful.

Money is a "medium of exchange." What does that mean? Basically, *money* is anything that can be traded for *goods* (products, like a sandwich, or a video game, or a bicycle) or for *services* (like raking leaves, or taking the trash out).

Around 2,000 B.C., people started using small pieces of bronze for trading, based on weight. People knew that bronze was a valuable metal, so these pieces would be accepted from town to town. They were often made into the shape of cattle, since cows and bulls were recognized as being valuable, and were often bartered for goods and services. Some pieces were small enough to carry around, but a more valuable piece of bronze would have to be bigger—too big to carry easily.

Finally the first real coins were made, in Lydia, a powerful ancient kingdom that no longer exists, but was located in what is now part of the Republic of Turkey. King Ardys built a mint where precious metal was used to make coin-like objects. The king's workers would gather a metal called *electrum*, actually a natural combination of gold and silver, found in the mountains and streams near the mint. They

Did You Know?
A mint is a building where coins are made.

Goat for Sale or Trade!

would use fire to make the metal softer, drop the soft metal onto a plate, place a punch over it, and then hit the punch with a hammer—hard! The punch had a design on it, which would be struck into the metal. The resulting electrum pieces were not like the coins we use today (their sizes and weights were random, and so was the purity of the gold and silver, and they only had a design on one side), but they were close.

When Ardys's son Alyattes became king, he made rules so that the Lydia's coins would all have the same weight (168 grains, about the same as two quarter dollars), and also designs on both sides. The 168-grain coins were called *staters*. Later, Alyattes also had his mints make smaller coins.

When Alyattes' son Croesus became king of Lydia, he made what many people consider the first true official coins. Croesus said "No more electrum," and only allowed gold and silver for his coins. They also had an official design—a lion's head and a bull, symbolizing the strength of his empire. This official design guaranteed that the coins were pure gold or pure silver, and authorized by the king.

Since then, coins have been struck by hundreds of kingdoms and other communities, in many metals, shapes, and sizes. In North America, people have used coins since colonial times, and the United States government has struck its own coins since the early 1790s, after the American Revolution. This book will introduce you to the fun hobby of collecting these interesting and valuable pieces of history.

Silver Half Stater of Lydia
This coin was struck sometime between 561 and 546 B.C., by order of King Croesus. Because these had a standard design, standard weight, and official stamp, they are among the first true coins as we define them today. (Actual size approximately 17 mm)

1795 Silver Dollar
This dollar was one of the first coins struck by the United States Mint. Today it's worth thousands of dollars!

oins have been around for nearly 3,000 years, which is why many people call coin collecting *the oldest hobby in the world*. Today, there are as many as 100 million coin collectors in the United States alone! Many of them started in the hobby by collecting state quarters struck by the U.S. Mint since 1999. There are coin shops, clubs, web sites, and conventions where people come from all over the world to buy, sell, trade, and talk about their hobby.

Did You Know?

A **numismatist** is a person who collects and studies money. This includes coins and paper currency, and also money-like objects such as tokens and medals. *Numismatics* is the study of coins and money. This is a popular hobby. More people belong to the American Numismatic Association than the entire population of Juneau, the capital city of Alaska!

Lots of kids collect coins. In fact, the American Numismatic Association (one of the largest coin clubs in the world) has a special group just for "Young Numismatists"— collectors age 13 to 22.

If you are a Boy Scout, you can earn your Coin Collecting Merit Badge. If you are a Girl Scout, you can earn your "Fun With Money" patch. Junior Girl Scouts can earn a "Collecting Hobbies" badge and Cadette Scouts can earn an interest patch for collecting coins, paper notes, or money-related items.

The American Numismatic Association can help you with the information you need to earn your Scout badge or patch. The Outreach Department helps ANA-member leaders conduct a "Coin Collecting Merit Badge Clinic," and the ANA's Young Numismatist (YN) programs provide special collecting information to help you earn your badge.

ANA Merit Badge Clinics are held twice a year, at the ANA National Money Show™ and the World's Fair of Money®. Clinics are also held at ANA Headquarters in Colorado Springs, Colorado. For more information you can email the ANA Outreach Department at outreach@money.org.

The Diversity of Coins

Coins come in many shapes and sizes. Most are round, but some are square, rectangular, or even triangular. There are even some coins from Somalia that are shaped like guitars! Some coins are tiny, like the silver three-cent piece made in the United States from 1851 to 1873. That little coin weighs less than a gram—about as much as a single paper clip. A much larger coin is the giant $50 gold commemorative struck in 1915 for the Panama-Pacific Exposition, to celebrate the opening of the Panama Canal. That coin weighs almost 84 grams—it's heavier than a handful of 30 dimes!

COINS CAN BE BIG
...like this 1915 Panama-Pacific commemorative $50 coin.

And coins can be little
...like this tiny silver three-cent piece.

Coins are also made of different metals, including gold, silver, copper, aluminum, brass, steel, bronze, and nickel. You can find coins in strange metals like goloid, zinc, and oroide. Some coins are even made out of two metals! These are called *bimetallic*. Canada has a bimetallic $2 coin. It has a central core made of bronze, which looks golden-brown, and an outer ring made of nickel, which looks silvery.

French 10-Francs Coin
The design of this French coin is called *Spirit of the Bastille*. The central part is made of nickel. The outer ring is mostly copper.

Coins in ancient times were like newspapers. They spread information throughout a kingdom or empire, and into other lands. Someone looking at a coin would be able to see a king's portrait, or find out about a war or battle commemorated on the coin, or learn about another country's culture and achievements.

Coins of the World
Coins are made in many different shapes and sizes, and of many different metals.

An Ancient Silver Coin From Corinth
Anyone who saw this coin would know it was from Corinth, because it shows Pegasus (the winged horse), who, according to legend, was captured by the Corinthian king.

A Modern Coin From the United States
On one side of this coin, the eagle in outer space symbolizes America's missions to the moon in the 1960s and 1970s.

Today you can hold a coin that was struck at the Mint this year, or one that was made hundreds of years ago! Think about the history behind these coins. Who knows? An Indian Head cent that was struck in the 1860s might have been in the pocket of President Abraham Lincoln. A Buffalo nickel from 1937 might have been used by an American soldier to buy a newspaper before he went to fight in Europe during World War II. And a nickel from 2004 shows us what the boat used by explorers Lewis and Clark looked like. Every coin, old or new, has a story to tell. That's part of what makes them fun to collect.

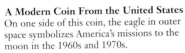

Talk Like a Coin Collector!

Obverse? Reverse? Motto? These are some things you'll find on every coin. Once you know the parts of a coin, you'll be able to talk about them with other collectors. Here's a guide to get you started.

Obverse (the Front of the Coin)

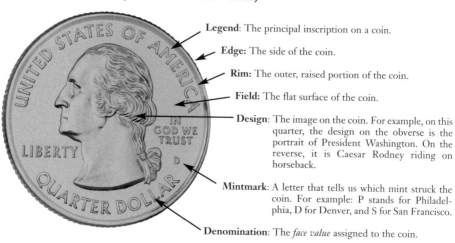

Legend: The principal inscription on a coin.

Edge: The side of the coin.

Rim: The outer, raised portion of the coin.

Field: The flat surface of the coin.

Design: The image on the coin. For example, on this quarter, the design on the obverse is the portrait of President Washington. On the reverse, it is Caesar Rodney riding on horseback.

Mintmark: A letter that tells us which mint struck the coin. For example: P stands for Philadelphia, D for Denver, and S for San Francisco.

Denomination: The *face value* assigned to the coin.

Reverse (the Back of the Coin)

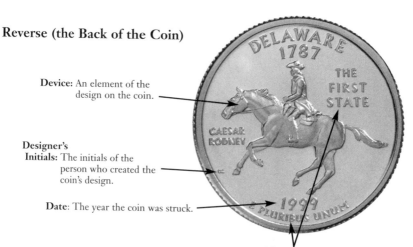

Device: An element of the design on the coin.

Designer's Initials: The initials of the person who created the coin's design.

Date: The year the coin was struck.

Motto: An inspirational legend on a coin. E PLURIBUS UNUM means ONE OUT OF MANY, which refers to one nation made out of many states. THE FIRST STATE is the nickname of Delaware.

oins are made by a country's government, which decides how many to make, what kinds to make, what they'll be made of, what they look like, and everything else about them. Most often a coin is designed by an artist who works for the government. Other times, the government will hold a contest so any artist can offer a design. Here are some famous coins that were made by designers who were picked through contests:

Jefferson Nickel

Bicentennial Quarter   Standing Liberty Quarter

Coins are made at government buildings called *mints*. Today, coins are struck by the United States Mint in Philadelphia and at two "branch mints," one in Denver and one in San Francisco. You can tell where a coin was struck by its *mintmark*—a little letter stamped on the coin (P for Philadelphia, or D for Denver).

In the past, coins were also struck at mints in other cities. Here is a list of every U.S. mint location and their mintmarks. Do you know which states they're located in? (The answers are on the next page.)

Mintmark	Which State?
C = Charlotte	_____
CC = Carson City	_____
D = Dahlonega (for gold coins)	_____
D = Denver	_____
O = New Orleans	_____
P = Philadelphia	_____
S = San Francisco	_____
W = West Point	_____

Stump Your Friends!

There was *another* mint that was run by the United States government—but not in the United States! The U.S. operated a mint in Manila, the capital city of the Philippines, from 1920 through 1941, when the islands were an American possession.

Some Philippine Coins
These are some of the coins struck in Manila by the United States government.

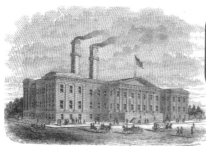

The San Francisco Mint as it appeared in 1874 when it was ready to be used for coinage. (*Banker's Almanac*)

Modern-Day Mintmarks
Today, you can find P and D mintmarks on coins in your pocket change.

The first Philadelphia Mint. Erected in 1792, it remained in use continuously through 1832.

Where Are the Mints Located?
Charlotte is in North Carolina.
Carson City is in Nevada.
Dahlonega is in Georgia.
Denver is in Colorado.
New Orleans is in Louisiana.
Philadelphia is in Pennsylvania.
San Francisco is in California.
West Point is in New York.
If you answered all eight correctly, you're a numismatic superstar. Ask a grownup and see if they can get them all right!

Types of U.S. Mint Coins

The U.S. Mint makes several kinds of coins.

CIRCULATION STRIKES

Circulation strikes (sometimes called *business strikes*) are regular coins that people use to buy and sell things. The Mint makes billions of these coins every year. Each coin is struck in a big machine called a *press*, and then dumped into a bin with thousands of other coins of the same denomination. Then they're counted, put into bags, and sent out to banks for distribution. The coins aren't handled very carefully, because they're made for business, not for collecting. The idea is to make lots of them as quickly as possible.

Steam-Powered Press, Used Starting in 1836
This machine could make 40,000 coins per day. Before that, the Mint's old hand-operated screw-action presses could only make 13,000 coins per day. Today the Philadelphia Mint can make *32 million* coins in a single day. Running full-time, it would take this steam-powered press more than two years to make that many coins, assuming it didn't break down first!

MINT SET COINS

Every year, the Mint makes some coins especially for collectors, and puts them into special packages as *Mint sets*. Each Mint set has one example of each denomination from each mint that made coins that year. Recent Mint sets have one cent, one nickel, one dime, one each of the five state quarters for that year, one half dollar, and one dollar from Philadelphia, plus one of each coin from Denver. That's a total of 20 coins. These coins are made like normal circulation strikes, but after they are struck, they are placed into the sets instead of being dumped into bins with other coins.

Extra Coins in Our Mint Sets
The U.S. Mint actually made two different nickels each year in 2004 and 2005. In Mint sets from those years, you'll have 22 coins instead of 20—one extra nickel from Philadelphia, and one extra from Denver.

PROOF SET COINS

Every year, the Mint also makes special *Proof* coins for collectors. These coins use the same designs as circulation strikes, but they're made from special dies that are polished to give the coins reflective surfaces like mirrors. The dies are cleaned often (after every

15 to 25 impressions), and are replaced frequently so they don't wear out. The coin *blanks* (pieces of metal the Proof coins are struck from) are also cleaned and polished to assure quality. Proof coins are struck at high pressure and slow speed, two or more times per coin. Each finished Proof coin is individually inspected, and handled carefully with gloves or tongs. They also get a final inspection by packers before being sonically sealed into special plastic cases.

The end result? Beautiful, flawless examples of America's coins—numismatic perfection!

COMMEMORATIVE COINS

Commemorative coins have been popular since the days of the Greeks and Romans. In the beginning they recorded and honored important events and people. There were no newspapers back then, and commemorative coins were useful in passing along news of the day.

Many modern nations have issued commemorative coins, and numismatists enjoy collecting them. Many American collectors feel the commemoratives of the United States are the most beautiful in the world. Collectors in other countries might feel the same way about *their* commemoratives!

Did You Know?

Commemorate comes from the Latin word that means "to remind." A commemorative coin reminds us of an important person, place, or event.

An Ancient Commemorative Coin
This denarius, a coin from ancient Rome, was struck in 54 B.C. to celebrate the defeat of King Aretas in Judaea, in the Roman province of Syria. It shows the king kneeling next to a camel and holding an olive branch, the symbol of peace. (Actual size 18 mm)

A More Recent Commemorative Coin
This half dollar from 1995 honors the soldiers of the American Civil War, and commemorates the battlefields they fought on.

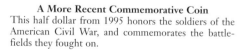

*H*ow much is a half dollar worth? That might be a trick question. A coin can have several kinds of value.

Every coin has a *face value*, or *denomination*. This is how much the coin is worth as spending money. For example, the face value of a half dollar is fifty cents, enough to buy a couple big gumballs in the machine at the supermarket. A coin's face value is guaranteed by the federal government. You will *always* be able to spend a half dollar for fifty cents!

A coin can also have *intrinsic value*. This is the value of the metal that makes up the coin—how much it would be worth if you melted it down. A modern half dollar is made of copper and nickel, two inexpensive metals. The coin's intrinsic value is maybe eight cents. An older half dollar has an intrinsic value of $2.70, because it's made out of silver, a much more valuable metal.

Modern *Copper-Nickel* Half Dollar   **Older *Silver* Half Dollar**

A third kind of value a coin can have is its *numismatic value*. This is how much it's worth to a coin collector. Numismatic value depends on how rare the coin is, the condition it's in (called its *grade*), how many people like to collect it, and other factors.

1892 Barber Half Dollar

Fewer than one million Barber half dollars were struck in 1892. That means this coin is old and fairly rare. In Mint State (with no traces of wear or damage), its numismatic value is about $1,000.

1952 Franklin Half Dollar

More than 21 million Franklin half dollars were struck in 1952. That's a lot of coins! Because this one is fairly common, its numismatic value is about $20 in Mint State.

*Y*ou should always handle coins carefully. Even though they're made of metal, they can be damaged by dirt, or dropping, or moisture, or other factors. Here are some guidelines on proper handling, lighting, and magnification.

PROPER HANDLING

1. Examine your coin over a soft surface, so it doesn't get damaged if you accidentally drop it. Always handle a coin by the edge, held between your fingertips. Never touch its surface. Oil, acid, and dirt from your fingertips can damage a coin and leave ugly fingerprints. This will lower your coin's value. Some collectors wear cotton gloves when they examine their coins, especially higher-grade examples. With proper care, your bare fingers should be fine.

2. Do not hold a coin near your mouth while you talk. Small drops of moisture that land on the coin's surface can cause spots on the surface.

3. Hold the coin at an angle, so that light from the bulb above reflects from the coin's surface into your eye. Turn and rotate the coin so you can observe its details from all angles. You should also examine the edge.

4. You will find that scratches or *hairlines* that are visible at one angle may become invisible when the coin is rotated. Take your time. Don't be in a hurry. Enjoy the beauty of your coin.

PROPER LIGHTING

Viewed under five different lighting conditions, a single coin can have five completely different appearances. Use a strong lamp light to observe your coins. Look at them in an area free of light from sources other than your lamp.

PROPER MAGNIFICATION

As with lighting, proper magnification can reveal much about a coin, including flaws that are hidden to the naked eye. Use a magnifying glass of at least three power (3x) and up to eight power (8x) strength. This will reveal scratches and other marks.

Visit a hobby shop

...and try out several magnifying glasses to find one that's comfortable and easy for you to use. Select a magnifying glass that's wide enough so you can study a fairly large amount of the coin's surface at one time. Over time the lens in a glass will become dusty or dirty. Be sure to clean it regularly (being careful not to injure the surface).

Magnifier (Loupe)

An H.E. Harris magnifier (or *loupe*, pronounced "loop") is a common sight at coin shows. You will see dealers and collectors slip them out of their pocket to examine interesting coins. (Some wear them on a chain or string around their neck, for constant easy access.) These magnifiers fold into their chrome cases to protect the lens, which is usually 10x to 16x or greater strength.

*I*n the sixth edition of the *Official American Numismatic Association Grading Standards for United States Coins*, numismatist Kenneth Bressett says:

> Grading is really very simple. All you need is four things:
> 1. a good magnifying glass,
> 2. a good light,
> 3. a good memory, and
> 4. 20 years of experience.

It's a good thing Mr. Bressett was just joking—or only grownups would be able to grade coins!

Getting Started

Obviously, you shouldn't have to wait 20 years before you jump into coin collecting. One of the best ways to learn about coins in general is by reading—and you're off to a good start with this book. After this, you can read a beginner's book devoted to grading, such as *The Whitman Insider Guide to Grading United States Coins*. When you're ready for a more advanced book, you can look into a book such as the *Official ANA Grading Standards*. These guides show photographs of a coin in a particular grade, with a text description of its appearance in that grade. By comparing your coin to the photos and text, you will be able to confidently grade your coin.

When it comes to grading coins, the more you look at, the better. This will make you familiar with how coins look in different conditions.

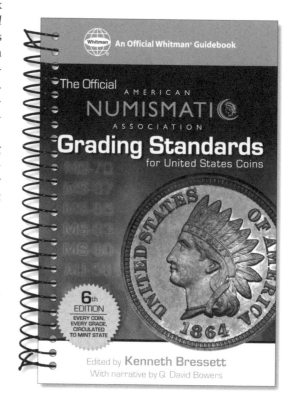

The Official ANA Grading Standards for United States Coins
"The official ANA grading system is used by collectors, dealers, and investors throughout the world," says noted numismatic researcher Bill Fivaz.

Practice, Practice, Practice

Reach into your pocket and take out the coins you have there. Or dump out your piggy bank. Or ask your mom or dad to go to a local bank and buy a few wrapped rolls of common modern coins—cents, nickels, dimes, quarters, or half dollars.

Now, examine these coins carefully. You will see some in bright Mint State, with very few marks, as well as some older coins that are well worn. By looking at hundreds of modern coins, you will see differences in mint luster, strike, and other grading factors. Think of this as a free education—you can always spend your "class materials" when you're done with them!

Once you've had some practice with common modern coins, you can concentrate on a single older series or type, such as Liberty Walking half dollars, Morgan silver dollars, or Buffalo nickels. Go to a coin show and examine every Buffalo nickel you can, from low-grade, worn examples to high-grade coins with bright luster. Ask questions. Soon, from this "field work," you'll have a good feel for the series.

These photographs show Buffalo nickels in three grades (out of a possible 70): MS-65, EF-45, and AG-3. You'll find more on these letter-and-number abbreviations in the next chapter.

Buffalo Nickel in Mint State
In Mint State, a Buffalo nickel has no trace of wear, though it may have slight blemishes such as hard-to-see nicks. The details in the Indian's portrait and the bison are sharp and complete. In higher grades of Mint State, it will have its original mint luster.

Buffalo Nickel in Extremely Fine Condition
In Extremely Fine condition, a Buffalo nickel shows slight wear on the hair above the braid, the temple, and the hair near the cheekbone. On the reverse, the high points of the bison's hip and thigh are lightly worn. The horn is sharp and nearly complete.

Buffalo Nickel in About Good Condition
In About Good condition, a Buffalo nickel is very worn, with parts of the date, legend, and details worn smooth. The design is outlined. The letters will merge into the coin's rims. This is a nickel that saw a lot of hand-to-hand circulation!

A non-collector might assume a description of "Good" means a coin is well preserved and very desirable. However, a numismatist knows that "Good" is one of the lowest grades, and that a coin in this condition is well worn, with most of its details gone.

Exactly how much wear does the coin have? How many marks or dings are on its surface? Does it have any of its original mint luster? These are questions that coin collectors think about when they grade coins. The ANA uses a 70-point grading system, where 70 is perfection, and 1 is the worst condition.

Proof Coin Grades

Proof refers to the way a coin is made, and is not a grade itself. A Proof is a coin made specially at the Mint as a souvenir or collectible. They are classified from PF-70 (perfection) down to PF-60. Three typical levels of Proof:

PF-65—A Proof-65 coin (abbreviated as PF-65, and sometimes called "gem Proof") has brilliant surfaces with no noticeable blemishes or flaws. It may have a few scattered, barely noticeable marks or hairlines.

PF-63—A Proof-63 coin (abbreviated as PF-63, and sometimes called "choice Proof") has reflective surfaces with only a few blemishes in secondary focal places. It has no major flaws.

PF-60—A Proof-60 coin (abbreviated as PF-60, with no special adjective) may have a surface with several contact marks, hairlines, or light rubs. Its surface may be dull and it might lack eye appeal.

Circulation-Strike Coin Grades

A circulation-strike coin (sometimes called a *business strike*) is any coin minted for commerce. These start out in Mint State at the moment they're pushed from the coinage press. Another word for Mint State is Uncirculated (abbreviated as Unc). Gradually a coin will wear down, as it is spent from hand to hand, to About Good condition.

Commonly encountered grading levels on the ANA's 70-point grading scale:

MS-70—An MS-70 coin (sometimes described as *Perfect Uncirculated*) is in perfect new condition, showing no trace of wear. This is the finest possible quality, with no scratches or marks. Very few regular-issue coins are ever found in this condition.

MS-65—An MS-65 coin (often described commercially as *Gem Uncirculated*) is an above-average Uncirculated example. It might be brilliant or lightly toned, and has very few contact marks on the surface or rim. MS-67 through MS-62 indicate slightly higher or lower grades of preservation.

MS-63—An MS-63 coin (often described as *Choice Uncirculated*) has some distracting contact marks or blemishes in prime focal areas. Its luster might not be as nice as a higher-grade coin.

MS-60—An MS-60 coin (typically described simply as *Uncirculated* or *Mint State*) has no trace of wear, but may show a number of contact marks. Its surface may be spotted or lack some luster.

AU-55—An AU-55 coin (*Choice About Uncirculated*, in the ANA's words) has evidence of rubbing on the high points of its design. Most of its mint luster remains.

AU-50—An AU-50 coin (*About Uncirculated*) has traces of light wear on many of its high points. At least half of the mint luster is still present.

EF-45—An EF-45 coin (*Choice Extremely Fine*) has light overall wear on its highest points. All design details are very sharp. Some of the mint luster is evident.

EF-40—An EF-40 coin (*Extremely Fine*) has light wear throughout the design, but all its features are sharp and well defined. Traces of luster may show.

VF-30—A VF-30 coin (*Choice Very Fine*) has light, even wear on the surface and highest parts of its design. All of its lettering and major features are sharp.

VF-20—A VF-20 coin (*Very Fine*) has moderate wear on the high points of its design. All major details are clear.

F-12—An F-12 coin (*Fine*) has moderate to considerable even wear. Its entire design is bold with an overall pleasing appearance.

VG-8—A VG-8 coin (*Very Good*) is well worn, with its main features clear and bold, although rather flat.

G-4—A G-4 coin (*Good*) is heavily worn, with its design visible but faint in areas. Many details are flat.

AG-3—An AG-3 coin (*About Good*) is very heavily worn, with portions of its lettering, date, and legend worn smooth. The date may be barely readable.

*T*his chapter shows you how to grade one of the most popular United States coin series: Liberty Walking half dollars, struck from 1916 to 1947. Study the photos, read the descriptions, and, if you own an example of this coin, compare it to what you see here. Soon you will have a good understanding of what to look for as you grade.

MINT STATE

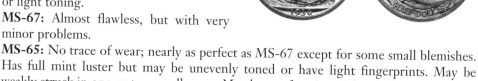

A Mint State Liberty Walking half dollar has no trace of wear.

MS-70: A flawless coin exactly as it was minted, with no trace of wear or damage. Must have full mint luster and brilliance or light toning.

MS-67: Almost flawless, but with very minor problems.

MS-65: No trace of wear; nearly as perfect as MS-67 except for some small blemishes. Has full mint luster but may be unevenly toned or have light fingerprints. May be weakly struck in one or two small spots. May have a few tiny nicks or marks.

MS-63: A Mint State coin with attractive mint luster, but noticeable contact marks or minor blemishes.

MS-60: An Uncirculated coin with no trace of wear, but with blemishes more obvious than for MS-63. May lack full mint luster, and surface may be dull, spotted, or heavily toned. A few small spots may be weakly struck.

ABOUT UNCIRCULATED

An About Uncirculated Liberty Walking half dollar has small traces of wear visible on its highest design points.

AU-58 (Very Choice AU): Has some signs of rubbing. On the obverse, check the hair above Liberty's temple, the right arm, and the left breast. On the reverse, check the high points of the eagle's head, breast, legs, and wings.

AU-55 (Choice AU): Much of the mint luster is still present, but often lightly worn in the obverse right field. The obverse shows only a trace of wear on the highest points of the head, breast, and right arm. The reverse shows a trace of wear below the eagle's neck, and on the left leg between the breast and left wing.

AU-50: Some mint luster is still present. The obverse shows traces of wear on the head, breast, arms, and left leg. The reverse shows traces of wear on high points of the wings and at the center of the head. All leg feathers are visible.

EXTREMELY FINE

An Extremely Fine Liberty Walking half dollar has very light wear on only its highest design points.

EF-45 (Choice): Part of the mint luster is still present. The obverse shows light wear spots on the head, breast, arms, left leg, and foot. Nearly all gown lines are clearly visible.

Sandal details are bold and complete. The knee is lightly worn but full and rounded. On the reverse, small flat spots show on high points of the eagle's breast and legs. The wing feathers have nearly full details.

EF-40: Traces of mint luster may still show. On the obverse, wear shows on the head, breast, arms, and left leg. Nearly all gown lines are visible. Sandal details are complete. The breast and knee are nearly flat. On the reverse, the high points of the eagle are lightly worn. Half the breast and leg feathers are visible. Central parts of the feathers below the neck are well worn.

VERY FINE

A Very Fine Liberty Walking half dollar has light to moderate even wear. All major features are sharp.

VF-30 (Choice): On the obverse, wear spots show on the head, breast, arms, and legs. The left leg is rounded but worn from above the knee to the ankle. The gown line crossing the body is partially visible. The knee is flat. The outline of the breast can be seen. On the reverse, the breast and legs of the eagle are moderately worn but clearly separated, with some feathers visible between them. The feather ends and folds are clearly visible in the right wing. The pupil of the eye is visible.

VF-20: On the obverse, the left leg is worn nearly flat. Wear spots show on the head, breast, arms, and foot. The breast is outlined. On the reverse, the entire eagle is lightly worn, but most major details are visible. The breast, central part of the legs, and top edge of the right wing are worn flat.

FINE

A Fine Liberty Walking half dollar has moderate to heavy even wear. Its entire design is clear and bold.

F-12: On the obverse, the gown stripes are worn but show clearly (except for pre-1921 coins, on which only half are visible). The right leg is lightly worn. The left leg is nearly flat and the sandal is worn but visible. The center of the body is worn, but some of the gown is visible. On the reverse, the breast is worn smooth. Half the wing feathers are visible although well worn in spots. The top two layers of feathers are visible in the left wing. The rim is full.

VERY GOOD

A Very Good Liberty Walking half dollar is well worn. Its design is clear but flat and lacking details.

VG-8: On the obverse, the entire design is weak. Most details in the gown are worn

smooth (except for coins after 1921, on which half the stripes must show). The date and all letters are clear, but the top of the motto may be weak. The rim is complete. The drapery across the body is partially visible. On the reverse, about one third of the feathers are visible, and the large feathers at the ends of the wings are well separated. The eagle's eye is visible. The rim is full and all letters are clear.

GOOD

A Good Liberty Walking half dollar is heavily worn. Its design and legend are visible but faint in spots.

G-4: On the obverse, the entire design is well worn, with very little detail remaining. The legend and date are weak but visible. The top of the date may be worn flat. The rim is flat but nearly complete. On the reverse, the eagle is worn nearly flat but is completely outlined. The lettering and motto are worn but clearly visible.

ABOUT GOOD

An About Good Liberty Walking half dollar shows only the outline of its design. Parts of the date and legend are worn smooth.

AG-3: On the obverse, the figure of Miss Liberty is outlined, with nearly all details worn away. The legend is visible but half worn away. The date is weak but readable. The rim merges with the lettering. On the reverse, the entire design is partially worn away. The letters merge with the rim.

ne of the oldest and best ways of starting a coin collection is by picking coins from circulation—the ones you get in pocket change. For example, you will be able to find most of the state quarters in change, or from coins your mom or dad bring home. If you need a certain state quarter and a friend has two of them, maybe he'll trade you one for another in *your* collection! (Remember how people used to *barter*, like the vegetable farmer who wanted a goat in this book's introduction?) The best part about collecting coins from circulation is that they only cost you their face value.

Do you have a friend or relative who is going to another country for vacation or business? You might ask them to bring back a few coins for your collection!

Most rare coins aren't easy to find in pocket change. To collect them, you will have to buy them at a coin shop, from the U.S. Mint, at a coin show, through the mail, or someplace else. (Or you might get them as presents from relatives and friends who know you collect coins.) Before you start buying coins, learn about them by reading a book or two. For United States coins, the *Guide Book of United States Coins*, often called the Red Book, is a good place to start. It tells about every U.S. coin minted since colonial times.

By reading about a coin—how rare it is, how to grade it, how much it's worth in different grades—you will have a good start for when you start looking to buy.

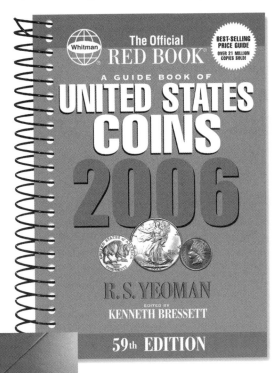

*Y*our coins are valuable, even if they're only worth face value. It's important to protect them and store them correctly so they don't get damaged. You can store them in ways that will display them, so your friends and family can see them and learn about them. Some of the ways to store your coins include folders, albums, cardboard holders, and hard plastic holders. As always, handle them carefully when you store them.

Folders

There are many coin folders for storing your collection. People have been putting their coins in folders for almost a hundred years; it's a very popular way to store and display them. If you go to a coin shop, bookstore, or hobby shop, you will find folders for every kind of U.S. coin, from copper half cents to gold pieces.

Each folder has openings where you can insert your coins—one for each date and mintmark. The idea is to fill each opening as you find (or buy) more coins for your collection, and after a while you'll have the entire folder filled up! This can take many weeks, months, or even years. The challenge of finding one of every date is part of the fun of collecting.

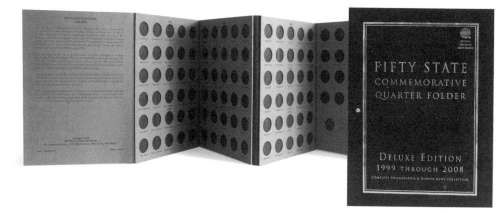

Some folders are fancy, like this map folder for state quarters. It has information about each state, plus pictures and a map of the whole country. This is a good way to display your collection, and you can easily see which coins you still need.

Coin folders are a durable and attractive way to store your collection, and most of them cost only a few dollars each.

Albums

With a *folder*, you can only see one side of each coin—the side facing out. With an *album*, you can see both sides. Coin albums look like fancy books that you can keep your collection in. They have removable plastic slides that protect both sides of your coins.

Cardboard Holders

At a coin show, you will often see coins in 2"x2" cardboard holders with clear windows. These are a cheap, easy way to store your coins and protect them from dust, fingerprints, and other things that can damage them.

2"x2" cardboard holders (often called *two by twos*) have windows of different sizes for different coins. Place your coin in the middle, fold it over, and then staple all four sides. Now you can look at both sides of your coin. You can write on the cardboard (for example, the year of the coin, its grade, how much you paid for it, etc.).

Coins in 2"x2" cardboard holders are easy to store in boxes. In fact, you can buy long cardboard boxes made just for storing them. You can also buy vinyl pages that have special sleeves for holding 2"x2" cardboard holders. These fit into a three-ring binder so you can look at your collection like a book.

Hard Plastic Holders

The best protection for your coins comes from hard plastic holders. These usually measure 2"x2", like a cardboard holder, and are big enough for a single coin. Some are longer, with openings for several coins. You put your coin in the opening in the middle and then click the two plastic halves together to hold it.

Another kind of plastic holder is a coin *tube*. These are clear or frosty holders that store a certain number of coins of a particular type—for example, 40 quarters, or 40 nickels, or 50 cents.

Storage Tips for Your Coins

You should store your coins in a dry place. Dampness will result in oxidation (like rust) or, in extreme cases, surface corrosion.

You can best avoid dampness by moving your coins to a drier location. If this is not possible, then put a packet of silica gel (available in drugstores or photography supply shops) in with the coins, and replace it regularly. This will absorb moisture. Also, storing your coins in airtight containers will help.

The more a coin is exposed to freely circulating air, the more likely it is to change color or to tone. Storing your coins in protective envelopes and hard plastic holders will usually (but not always) help prevent this.

Do not buy any coin storage containers unless you know what they're made of. A few years ago clear flexible plastic envelopes or "flips" were very popular for storing coins. These were made of a plastic called PVC. Some albums were made of this material as well. Over time, PVC can form a harmful goo that can damage the surfaces of your coins.

Another important tip related to storing and preserving your collection: even if a coin is dirty or toned, you should not try to clean it. Cleaning with polishes, pastes, or other chemicals can strip a coin of its natural luster. This will make it less valuable.

S tate quarters: since 1999, everybody has been talking about them!

Today, these wonderful state-reverse quarter dollars have captured the attention and interest of just about every collector. Millions of people—some who consider themselves serious numismatists, and others who just like to collect these neat coins— eagerly check their pocket change to see what's new, to find a coin honoring New York, California, Texas, or whichever state they live in, or to see the latest designs.

Each year since 1999 the United States Mint has issued five new designs, each featuring a different state, in the order in which the states joined the Union. In the pages to follow you will learn all about these fascinating coins—remarkable in their diversity, unequalled in their historical importance, and inexpensive enough that anyone can afford to collect them.

Basic Facts (FOR ALL STATE QUARTERS, 1999 TO DATE)

Designer: The obverse was originally designed by John Flanagan, whose initials JF are on President Washington's neck. The portrait was changed in 1999 by William Cousins, who added many new hair details. In that year the initials WC were added to those of Flanagan, now appearing run together as JFWC. For the reverses, many different designers and Mint engravers worked on the coins.

The state quarter obverse is the same for every coin in the series, except for the date change every year. This design is different from the quarters of 1932 to 1998. In 1999, to make room for the creative designs on the reverse of the state quarters, the inscriptions UNITED STATES OF AMERICA and QUARTER DOLLAR were relocated to the obverse, above and below the portrait. LIBERTY and IN GOD WE TRUST were moved to new positions.

Compare the Two Designs
How many differences can you see?

 Specifications (clad issues): *Composition:* Outer layers of copper-nickel (75% copper and 25% nickel) bonded to an inner core of pure copper. The copper is visible by viewing the coin edge-on. • *Diameter:* 24.3 mm • *Weight:* 5.67 grams • *Edge:* Reeded

 Specifications (silver issues): *Composition:* 90% silver; 10% copper • *Diameter:* 24.3 mm • *Weight:* 6.25 grams • *Edge:* Reeded

Delaware

THE FIRST STATE

Delaware became our 1st state on December 7, 1787. The ★ capital is Dover. Delaware gets its name from one of Virginia's early governors, Lord De La Warr. Delaware is the only state with no National Parks and is only nine miles wide at its narrowest point.

Delaware's state bird, the Blue Hen Chicken, was chosen because, during the Revolutionary War, soldiers compared their military strength to that of these aggressive birds.

- CAPITAL... Dover

- STATE TREE... American Holly

- LAND AREA... 1,955 sq. mi.

- RANK IN SIZE (land area)... 49th

- STATE SONG... "Our Delaware"

- LARGEST CITY... Wilmington

BLUE HEN CHICKEN
PEACH BLOSSOM

STATE SEAL

STATE FLAG

Pennsylvania
SECOND STATE

RUFFED GROUSE
MOUNTAIN LAUREL

STATE SEAL

STATE FLAG

Pennsylvania became our 2nd state on December 12, 1787. The ★ capital is Harrisburg. Pennsylvania was named for Admiral William Penn, father of the state's founder. Philadelphia was once the nation's capital. The first commercial radio broadcast originated from Pittsburgh. Pennsylvania was the birthplace of President James Buchanan as well as the first state to put its website address on its license plates.

- CAPITAL... Harrisburg

- STATE TREE... Hemlock

- LAND AREA... 44,820 sq. mi.

- RANK IN SIZE (land area)... 32nd

- STATE SONG... "Pennsylvania"

- LARGEST CITY... Philadelphia

New Jersey

GARDEN STATE

New Jersey became our 3rd state on December 18, 1787. The ★ capital is Trenton. New Jersey is one of the most crowded of the 50 states, with more than 1,000 people per square mile. It is the only state where every single county is classified as a metropolitan area. Vacation spot Atlantic City has the longest boardwalk in the world. New Jersey was the birthplace of President Grover Cleveland. Hungry for a burger? New Jersey is considered the diner capital of the world.

EASTERN GOLDFINCH   STATE SEAL
VIOLET

- CAPITAL…Trenton

- STATE TREE… Red Oak

- LAND AREA… 7,419 sq. mi.

- RANK IN SIZE (land area)… 46th

- STATE SONG… "Ode To
                New Jersey"

- LARGEST CITY… Newark

STATE FLAG

Georgia

EMPIRE STATE OF THE SOUTH

BROWN THRASHER
CHEROKEE ROSE   STATE SEAL

eorgia became our 4th state on January 2, 1788. The ★ capital is Atlanta. Georgia is named after England's King George II. Georgia is the largest state east of the Mississippi and America's number one producer of peanuts and pecans. The first gold rush in the U.S. took place in northern Georgia in 1828 when gold was discovered near Dahlonega. Georgia is also the home state of President Jimmy Carter.

STATE FLAG

- CAPITAL... Atlanta

- STATE TREE... Live Oak

- LAND AREA... 57,919 sq. mi.

- RANK IN SIZE (land area)... 21st

- STATE SONG... "Georgia On My Mind"

- LARGEST CITY... Atlanta

Connecticut

CONSTITUTION STATE

onnecticut became our 5th state on January 9, 1788. The ★ capital is Hartford. Connecticut is an Algonquin and Mohican word meaning "place beside a long river." This place has produced some famous residents. Among them are circus pioneer P.T. Barnum, actress Katherine Hepburn, linguist Noah Webster, abolitionist John Brown, and President George W. Bush. The first atomic submarine was built in Connecticut. Our 5th state was one of only two states that never ratified the 18th amendment for prohibition.

ROBIN
MOUNTAIN LAUREL

STATE SEAL

- CAPITAL… Hartford

- STATE TREE… White Oak

- LAND AREA… 4,845 sq. mi.

- RANK IN SIZE (land area)… 48th

- STATE SONG… "Yankee Doodle"

- LARGEST CITY… Bridgeport

STATE FLAG

Massachusetts

THE BAY STATE

Massachusetts became our 6th state on February 6, 1788. The ★ capital is Boston. In the Massachusett Indian language, the name meant "large hill place." Many presidents were born in Massachusetts: John Adams, John Quincy Adams, John F. Kennedy, and George Bush. Massachusetts also claims many firsts. The first subway was built in Boston in 1897; the first U.S. Postal code is Agawam, 01001; and Harvard was the first college in the country, founded in 1636. Of course, the state dessert is Boston Cream Pie.

CHICKADEE
MAYFLOWER

STATE SEAL

- CAPITAL... Boston

- STATE TREE... American Elm

- LAND AREA... 7,838 sq. mi.

- RANK IN SIZE (land area)... 45th

- STATE SONG... "All Hail to Massachusetts"

- LARGEST CITY... Boston

STATE FLAG

Maryland

OLD LINE STATE

Maryland became our 7th state on April 28, 1788. The ★ capital is Annapolis, which once served as the capital of the United States. Maryland even gave up some of its land to help found Washington, D.C. The name Maryland was a tribute to Henrietta Maria, wife of King Charles I. Maryland is home to the U.S. Naval Academy and is the only state pronounced as a compound word. The state flag features the crests of Maryland's two founding families.

- CAPITAL... Annapolis

- STATE TREE... White Oak

- LAND AREA... 9,775 sq. mi.

- RANK IN SIZE (land area)... 42nd

- STATE SONG... "Maryland, My Maryland"

- LARGEST CITY... Baltimore

BALTIMORE ORIOLE
BLACK-EYED SUSAN

STATE SEAL

STATE FLAG

South Carolina

THE PALMETTO STATE

S outh Carolina became our 8th state on May 23, 1788. The ★ capital is Columbia. Charleston, named after King Charles II, was the site of the first battle in the Civil War. President Andrew Jackson was born in South Carolina, which is also home to Upper Whitewater Falls, the highest waterfall in the east. The state flower is the Yellow Jessamine, and the state dance is none other than the Shag.

GREAT
CAROLINA WREN
YELLOW JESSAMINE

STATE SEAL

- CAPITAL... Columbia

- STATE TREE... Palmetto

- LAND AREA... 30,111 sq. mi.

- RANK IN SIZE (land area)... 40th

- STATE SONG... "Carolina"

- LARGEST CITY... Columbia

STATE FLAG

New Hampshire

THE GRANITE STATE

ew Hampshire became our 9th state on June 21, 1788. The ★ capital is Concord. Hampshire County was the English home of state co-founder Captain John Mason; this gives New Hampshire its name. New Hampshire was the first state to declare independence from England. Fittingly, the state motto is "Live Free or Die." President Franklin Pierce was born in New Hampshire.

PURPLE FINCH
PURPLE LILAC

STATE SEAL

- CAPITAL... Concord

- STATE TREE... White Birch

- LAND AREA... 8,969 sq. mi.

- RANK IN SIZE (land area)... 44th

- STATE SONG... "Old New
                Hampshire"

- LARGEST CITY... Manchester

STATE FLAG

Virginia

OLD DOMINION STATE

irginia became our 10th state on June 25, 1788. The ★ capital is Richmond. Virginia got its name from England's "Virgin Queen," Elizabeth I. Jamestown was the first settlement in the United States. Two wars ended in Virginia: the American Revolution (when Cornwallis surrendered in Yorktown) and the Civil War (when Lee surrendered at Appomattox Courthouse). Eight American presidents were born in Virginia: George Washington, Thomas Jefferson, James Madison, James Monroe, William H. Harrison, John Tyler, Zachary Taylor, and Woodrow Wilson.

CARDINAL
DOGWOOD

STATE SEAL

- CAPITAL... Richmond

- STATE TREE... American Dogwood

- LAND AREA... 39,598 sq. mi.

- RANK IN SIZE (land area)... 37th

- STATE SONG... "Carry Me Back
  To Old Virginia"

- LARGEST CITY... Virginia Beach

STATE FLAG

New York

EMPIRE STATE

*N*ew York became our 11th state on July 26, 1788. The ★ capital is Albany. New York is named after England's Duke of York. Four presidents were born in New York: Martin Van Buren, Millard Fillmore, Theodore Roosevelt, and Franklin Delano Roosevelt. The *New York Post* is the oldest running paper in the United States. There are more than 1,300 museums and galleries and 230 theaters in New York.

BLUEBIRD   STATE SEAL
ROSE

- CAPITAL... Albany

- STATE TREE... Sugar Maple

- LAND AREA... 47,224 sq. mi.

- RANK IN SIZE (land area)... 30th

- STATE SONG... "I Love New York"

- LARGEST CITY... New York City

STATE FLAG

North Carolina

THE TARHEEL STATE

CARDINAL
AMERICAN DOGWOOD

STATE SEAL

STATE FLAG

North Carolina became our 12th state on November 21, 1789. The ★ capital is Raleigh. This state was named after King Charles I. The nickname Tar Heel State originated during the Civil War when soldiers teased a cowardly regiment about needing tar to help them "stick it out" during battle. There are three mountain ranges in North Carolina: the Appalachian, the Blue Ridge, and the Great Smoky Mountains. Presidents James Polk and Andrew Johnson were born in North Carolina.

- CAPITAL... Raleigh

- STATE TREE... Pine

- LAND AREA... 48,718 sq. mi.

- RANK IN SIZE (land area)... 29th

- STATE SONG... "The Old North State"

- LARGEST CITY... Charlotte

Rhode Island

THE OCEAN STATE

R hode Island became our 13th state on May 29, 1790. The ★ capital is Providence. Our smallest state was named after the Dutch words for "red clay." Rhode Island made its political mark by refusing to ratify the U.S. Constitution without a Bill of Rights and by not ratifying the 18th amendment to the Constitution for prohibition. The state motto is Hope, the state flower is the Violet, and the state bird is the Rhode Island Red Hen.

RHODE ISLAND
RED HEN
VIOLET

STATE SEAL

• CAPITAL... Providence

• STATE TREE... Red Maple

• LAND AREA... 1,045 sq. mi.

• RANK IN SIZE (land area)... 50th

• STATE SONG... "Rhode Island, It's For Me"

• LARGEST CITY... Providence

STATE FLAG

Vermont

THE GREEN MOUNTAIN STATE

Vermont became our 14th state on March 4, 1791. The ★ capital is Montpelier. Vermont means "green mountain" in French. Two presidents were born in Vermont: Chester Arthur and Calvin Coolidge. Vermont was the first state admitted to the Union after the original 13 colonies. Vermont was also the first to outlaw slavery and the first U.S. patent was issued to a Vermonter.

HERMIT THRUSH
RED CLOVER

STATE SEAL

STATE FLAG

- CAPITAL... Montpelier

- STATE TREE... Sugar Maple

- LAND AREA... 9,249 sq. mi.

- RANK IN SIZE (land area)... 43rd

- STATE SONG... "These Green Mountains"

- LARGEST CITY... Burlington

Kentucky

THE BLUEGRASS STATE

entucky became our 15th state on June 1, 1792. The capital is Frankfort. Kentucky is an Iroquois word meaning "land of tomorrow." The state flag depicts two people acting out the state motto, "United We Stand, Divided We Fall." Kentucky is birthplace to U.S. President Abraham Lincoln and Confederate President Jefferson Davis. The oldest horse race in the country, the Kentucky Derby, takes place every year on the first Saturday in May.

- CAPITAL... Frankfort
- STATE TREE... Tulip Poplar
- LAND AREA... 39,732 sq. mi.
- RANK IN SIZE (land area)... 36th
- STATE SONG... "My Old Kentucky Home"
- LARGEST CITY... Louisville

CARDINAL
GOLDENROD

STATE SEAL

STATE FLAG

Tennessee

THE VOLUNTEER STATE

MOCKINGBIRD
IRIS

STATE SEAL

Tennessee became our 16th state on June 1, 1796. The ★ capital is Nashville. Tennessee is taken from "tanasi," the Cherokee word for "villages." The Grand Ole Opry is the longest running live radio program in the country, broadcast every week since 1925. The nickname, Volunteer State, was given because of the bravery of Tennessee's volunteer soldiers in the Battle of New Orleans in the War of 1812.

- CAPITAL... Nashville

- STATE TREE... Tulip Poplar

- LAND AREA... 41,220 sq. mi.

- RANK IN SIZE (land area)... 34th

- STATE SONG... "The Tennessee Waltz"

- LARGEST CITY... Memphis

STATE FLAG

43

Ohio

THE BUCKEYE STATE

*O*hio became our 17th state on March 1, 1803. The ★ capital is Columbus. Ohio, which means "good river" in Iroquois, is the birthplace of seven presidents: Grant, Hayes, Garfield, B. Harrison, McKinley, Taft, and Harding. Ohio gave us the first traffic light (1923), the first cash register (1878), and the first hot dog (1900). Interestingly, Ohioans have made their mark in space: Neil Armstrong was the first man to walk on the moon and John Glenn is the oldest man to fly in outer space to date.

- CAPITAL... Columbus
- STATE TREE... Buckeye
- LAND AREA... 40,953 sq. mi.
- RANK IN SIZE (land area)... 35th
- STATE SONG... "Beautiful Ohio"
- LARGEST CITY... Columbus

CARDINAL
SCARLET CARNATION

STATE SEAL

STATE FLAG

44

Louisiana

THE PELICAN STATE

EASTERN BROWN
PELICAN
MAGNOLIA

STATE SEAL

STATE FLAG

ouisiana became our 18th state on April 30, 1812. The ★ capital is Baton Rouge. Louisiana is named in honor of King Louis XIV and is the only state in the Union that has parishes instead of counties. Because of slow communication, the famous Battle of New Orleans was actually fought two weeks after the War of 1812 ended. Louisiana is one of the most racially and culturally diverse states, with French, Spanish, Cuban, and African influences.

- CAPITAL... Baton Rouge
- STATE TREE... Bald Cypress
- LAND AREA... 43,566 sq. mi.
- RANK IN SIZE (land area)... 33rd
- STATE SONG... "Give Me Louisiana"
- LARGEST CITY... New Orleans

Indiana

THE HOOSIER STATE

Indiana became our 19th state on December 11, 1816. The ★ capital is Indianapolis. The name of this state was created by Congress to symbolize the "land of the Indians." Indiana's official motto is The Crossroads of America, and it's known as the Hoosier State, a phrase associated with athletics but actually taken from a poem written in the 1930s.

- CAPITAL... Indianapolis
- STATE TREE... Tulip Tree
- LAND AREA... 35,870 sq. mi.
- RANK IN SIZE (land area)... 38th
- STATE SONG... "On The Banks of the Wabash"
- LARGEST CITY... Indianapolis

CARDINAL
PEONY

STATE SEAL

STATE FLAG

Mississippi
THE MAGNOLIA STATE

Mississippi became our 20th state on December 10, 1817. The ★ capital is Jackson. The name derives from the Chippewa words "mmici zibi," meaning "Father of Waters." The first lung and heart transplants were performed in Mississippi. Memorial Day was first celebrated in 1866 at the Friendship Cemetery in Columbus when the women of the town decorated both Union and Confederate graves to remember the dead.

MOCKINGBIRD
MAGNOLIA

STATE SEAL

- CAPITAL... Jackson

- STATE TREE... Magnolia

- LAND AREA... 46,914 sq. mi.

- RANK IN SIZE (land area)... 31st

- STATE SONG... "Go Mississippi"

- LARGEST CITY... Jackson

STATE FLAG

47

Illinois

THE LAND OF LINCOLN

Illinois became our 21st state on December 3, 1818. The ★ capital is Springfield. Illinois is an Algonquin word meaning "tribe of superior men." Illinois was the first state to ratify the 13th Amendment abolishing slavery. The tallest skyscraper in North America is the Sears Tower in Chicago. Illinois is the birthplace of President Ronald Reagan.

- CAPITAL... Springfield

- STATE TREE... White Oak

- LAND AREA... 55,593 sq. mi.

- RANK IN SIZE (land area)... 24th

- STATE SONG... "Illinois"

- LARGEST CITY... Chicago

CARDINAL
PURPLE VIOLET

STATE SEAL

STATE FLAG

Alabama

THE YELLOWHAMMER STATE

Alabama became our 22nd state on December 14, 1819. The ★ capital is Montgomery. In the Creek Indian language, Alabama means "tribal town." The state nickname, Yellowhammer State, dates back to the Civil War and refers to the new, bright yellow cloth that was used on soldiers' uniforms. Famous Alabamians include baseball player Hank Aaron and educator Helen Keller.

YELLOWHAMMER
CAMELLIA

STATE SEAL

- CAPITAL... Montgomery

- STATE TREE... Southern Pine

- LAND AREA... 50,750 sq. mi.

- RANK IN SIZE (land area)... 28th

- STATE SONG... "Alabama"

- LARGEST CITY... Birmingham

STATE FLAG

Maine

THE PINE TREE STATE

aine became our 23rd state on March 15, 1820. The ★ capital is Augusta. Maine is a reference to the "main land," as opposed to the offshore islands of that region. Maine is the only state with a one-syllable name and the only state that borders just one other state. Maine has so many deep harbors that all the navies in the world could drop anchor in them.

CHICKADEE
WHITE PINE CONE
AND TASSEL

STATE SEAL

- CAPITAL... Augusta

- STATE TREE... White Pine

- LAND AREA... 30,865 sq. mi.

- RANK IN SIZE (land area)... 39th

- STATE SONG... "State of
                Maine Song"

- LARGEST CITY... Portland

STATE FLAG

Missouri

THE SHOW ME STATE

BLUEBIRD
HAWTHORN

STATE SEAL

Missouri became our 24th state on August 10, 1821. The ★ capital is Jefferson City. Missouri is an Indian word meaning "town of large canoes." The Pony Express began in Missouri in 1860. Ice cream was invented at the 1904 World's Fair in Missouri. Harry S Truman was born in Missouri, as was TV newscaster Walter Cronkite and novelist Mark Twain. Entertainment visionary Walt Disney grew up in Missouri.

- CAPITAL... Jefferson City

- STATE TREE... Flowering Dogwood

- LAND AREA... 68,898 sq. mi.

- RANK IN SIZE (land area)... 18th

- STATE SONG... "Missouri Waltz"

- LARGEST CITY... Kansas City

STATE FLAG

Arkansas

THE NATURAL STATE

Arkansas became our 25th state on June 15th, 1836. The ★ capital is Little Rock.

The state gets its name from a Sioux word "acansa," meaning "downstream place."

The Arkansas flag sports a red diamond, representing that it is the only state in the nation where diamonds are actively mined. President Bill Clinton was born in Arkansas. To end the pronunciation debate, in 1881, the General Assembly resolved that Arkan-SAW is the correct way to say this state's name.

MOCKINGBIRD
APPLE BLOSSOM

STATE SEAL

- CAPITAL... Little Rock

- STATE TREE... Pine

- LAND AREA... 52,075 sq. mi.

- RANK IN SIZE (land area)... 27th

- STATE SONG... "Arkansas, Oh, Arkansas"

- LARGEST CITY... Little Rock

STATE FLAG

Michigan

THE WOLVERINE STATE

ichigan became our 26th state on January 26th, 1837. The ★ capital is Lansing. The state gets its name from the Chippewa word "meicigana," meaning "great or large lake." Michigan borders the largest of the Great Lakes. Michigan was the first state to guarantee every child in the state the right to a high school education.

ROBIN
APPLE BLOSSOM

STATE SEAL

- CAPITAL... Lansing

- STATE TREE... White Pine

- LAND AREA... 56,809 sq. mi.

- RANK IN SIZE (land area)... 22nd

- STATE SONG... "Michigan, My Michigan"

- LARGEST CITY... Detroit

STATE FLAG

Florida

THE SUNSHINE STATE

Florida became our 27th state on March 3, 1845. The ★ capital is Tallahassee. Explorer Ponce de Leon named Florida after the Pasqua de Flores, or "feast of flowers," that he celebrated on Easter, 1531. Even though people call Florida the Sunshine State, its real nickname is the Orange State because it is the nation's largest orange grower. It is also the place to go to see space launches from Cape Canaveral.

- CAPITAL... Tallahassee
- STATE TREE... Sabal Palmetto
- LAND AREA... 53,997 sq. mi.
- RANK IN SIZE (land area)... 26th
- STATE SONG... "Suwannee River"
- LARGEST CITY... Jacksonville

MOCKINGBIRD
ORANGE BLOSSOM

STATE SEAL

STATE FLAG

Texas

THE LONE STAR STATE

exas became our 28th state on December 29, 1845. The ★ capital is Austin. The name Texas comes from the word "tejas," meaning "friends and allies." Notable in Texas state history is that from 1836 to 1845 Texas was an independent nation. Today Texas claims 7.4% of the total area of the United States, making it the second largest state. Presidents Dwight D. Eisenhower and Lyndon B. Johnson were born in the Lone Star State.

MOCKINGBIRD
BLUEBONNET

STATE SEAL

- CAPITAL... Austin

- STATE TREE... Pecan

- LAND AREA... 261,914 sq. mi.

- RANK IN SIZE (land area)... 2nd

- STATE SONG... "Texas, Our Texas"

- LARGEST CITY... Houston

STATE FLAG

Iowa

THE HAWKEYE STATE

Iowa became our 29th state on December 28, 1846. The ★ capital is Des Moines. Iowa is from the Indian word "ayuxwa," meaning "one who soothes." President Herbert Hoover, a native Iowan, was the first president born west of the Mississippi. Iowa has a beautiful state rock, the geode. It's found in limestone nodules and when broken open reveals a lining of colorful quartz and crystals.

EASTERN GOLDFINCH
WILD PRAIRIE ROSE

STATE SEAL

- CAPITAL... Des Moines

- STATE TREE... Oak

- LAND AREA... 55,875 sq. mi.

- RANK IN SIZE (land area)... 23rd

- STATE SONG... "The Song of Iowa"

- LARGEST CITY... Des Moines

STATE FLAG

Wisconsin

THE BADGER STATE

ROBIN
WOOD VIOLET

STATE SEAL

STATE FLAG

Wisconsin became our 30th state on May 29, 1848. The ★ capital is Madison. In the Chippewa tongue, Wisconsin means "a grassy place." Wisconsin is the nation's leading milk producer. Over 1.5 million cows give enough milk to supply 42 million people for a year; that's not counting butter or cheese. The first kindergarten in the nation was started in Wisconsin in 1856.

- CAPITAL... Madison
- STATE TREE... Sugar Maple
- LAND AREA... 54,314 sq. mi.
- RANK IN SIZE (land area)... 25th
- STATE SONG... "On Wisconsin"
- LARGEST CITY... Milwaukee

California

THE GOLDEN STATE

California became our 31st state on September 9, 1850. The ★ capital is Sacramento. California was named after a mythical Spanish paradise. California's motto is Eureka, which translates as "I have found it!"—a perfect slogan for the gold rush. In Sequoia National Park there is a 3,500-year-old Redwood, and California's Mt. Whitney is the highest peak in the "lower 48." President Richard Nixon was born in California.

CALIFORNIA VALLEY QUAIL
GOLDEN POPPY

STATE SEAL

- CAPITAL... Sacramento

- STATE TREE... California Redwood

- LAND AREA... 155,973 sq. mi.

- RANK IN SIZE (land area)... 3rd

- STATE SONG... "I Love You, California"

- LARGEST CITY... Los Angeles

STATE FLAG

Minnesota

THE GOPHER STATE

COMMON LOON
PINK and WHITE
LADY'S-SLIPPER

STATE SEAL

innesota became our 32nd state on May 11, 1858. The ★ capital is St. Paul. Minnesota is Sioux for "sky-tinted water." Be careful; it's illegal to pick the state flower, a Pink and White Lady's-Slipper. Minnesotan baseball commentator Halsey Hal was the first to say "Holy Cow" in a broadcast. Many inventions have come from Minnesota including Scotch tape, HMOs, the stapler, and the bundt pan.

- CAPITAL... St. Paul

- STATE TREE... Norway Pine

- LAND AREA... 79,617 sq. mi.

- RANK IN SIZE (land area)... 14th

- STATE SONG... "Hail! Minnesota"

- LARGEST CITY... Minneapolis

STATE FLAG

Oregon

THE BEAVER STATE

Oregon became our 33rd state on February 14, 1859. The ★ capital is Salem. The origin of the word Oregon is unknown. Oregon is the only state with a flag that has two designs. The reverse side has a picture of a beaver. The deepest lake in the United States is Oregon's Crater Lake, formed by an ancient volcano. Another Oregon claim to fame is ghost towns—it has more than any other state.

- CAPITAL... Salem

- STATE TREE... Douglas Fir

- LAND AREA... 96,003 sq. mi.

- RANK IN SIZE (land area)... 10th

- STATE SONG... "Oregon, My Oregon"

- LARGEST CITY... Portland

WESTERN MEADOWLARK
OREGON GRAPE

STATE SEAL

STATE FLAG

Kansas

THE SUNFLOWER STATE

Kansas became our 34th state on January 29, 1861. The ★ capital is Topeka. The state name originated from an Indian word, "konza," meaning "people of the south wind." A Kansas county is the geographical center of the United States. Kansan Hattie McDaniel was the first African-American woman to win an Academy Award. The first woman mayor in the U.S. was elected in Kansas in 1887.

WESTERN MEADOWLARK
SUNFLOWER

STATE SEAL

- CAPITAL... Topeka

- STATE TREE... Cottonwood

- LAND AREA... 81,823 sq. mi.

- RANK IN SIZE (land area)... 13th

- STATE SONG... "Home on the Range"

- LARGEST CITY... Wichita

STATE FLAG

West Virginia

THE MOUNTAIN STATE

est Virginia became our 35th state on June 20, 1863. The ★ capital is Charleston. This state takes its name from the "Virgin Queen," Elizabeth I.

Mother's Day began in West Virginia and that's just one of many firsts. The first rural mail delivery, the first brick street, the first major battle of the Civil War, the first free school for African Americans, and the first state sales tax all originated in the Mountain State.

CARDINAL
RHODODENDRON

STATE SEAL

- CAPITAL... Charleston

- STATE TREE... Sugar Maple

- LAND AREA... 24,087 sq. mi.

- RANK IN SIZE (land area)... 41st

- STATE SONG... "The West Virginia Hills"

- LARGEST CITY... Huntington (Metropolitan Area)

STATE FLAG

Nevada

THE SILVER STATE

evada became our 36th state on October 31, 1864. The ★ capital is Carson City. Nevada means "snow capped" in Spanish. Nevada produces the most gold in the nation. The Nevada constitution was sent by telegram in Morse code from Carson City to Washington, D.C. in 1864. The transmission took hours. There are more hotel rooms in Las Vegas than anywhere else in the world.

MOUNTAIN BLUEBIRD
SAGEBRUSH

STATE SEAL

- CAPITAL… Carson City

- STATE TREE… Bristlecone Pine/ Single Leaf Piñon

- LAND AREA… 109,806 sq. mi.

- RANK IN SIZE (land area)… 7th

- STATE SONG… "Home Means Nevada"

- LARGEST CITY… Las Vegas

STATE FLAG

Nebraska

THE CORNHUSKER STATE

ebraska became our 37th state on March 1, 1867. The ★ capital is Lincoln. Nebraska gets its name from an Oto Indian word meaning "flat water." President Gerald Ford was born in the Cornhusker State, which is not a reference to hard farm work, but to the University of Nebraska athletic teams. The 911 emergency calling system was developed in Nebraska.

- CAPITAL... Lincoln

- STATE TREE... Cottonwood

- LAND AREA... 76,878 sq. mi.

- RANK IN SIZE (land area)... 15th

- STATE SONG... "Beautiful Nebraska"

- LARGEST CITY... Omaha

WESTERN MEADOWLARK
GOLDENROD

STATE SEAL

STATE FLAG

Colorado

THE CENTENNIAL STATE

LARK BUNTING
WHITE & LAVENDER
COLUMBINE

STATE SEAL

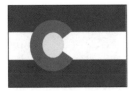

STATE FLAG

Colorado became our 38th state on August 1, 1876. The ★ capital is Denver. Colorado was originally a Spanish reference to the red rock around the Colorado River. The federal government owns one-third of the land in Colorado. This was the only state to ever turn down the opportunity to host an Olympics (1976). The United States Air Force Academy is located in Colorado.

- CAPITAL… Denver
- STATE TREE… Colorado Blue Spruce
- LAND AREA… 103,729 sq. mi.
- RANK IN SIZE (land area)… 8th
- STATE SONG… "Where The Columbines Grow"
- LARGEST CITY… Denver

North Dakota

THE FLICKERTAIL STATE

orth Dakota became our 39th state on November 2 1889. The ★ capital is Bismarck. Dakota is a Sioux word meaning "allies." The town of Rugby is the geographical center of the North American continent. The state legislature has twice tried to change the name of the state with no success. Before he was president, Theodore Roosevelt fought with a North Dakota regiment in the Spanish-American War.

- CAPITAL... Bismarck
- STATE TREE... American Elm
- LAND AREA... 68,994 sq. mi.
- RANK IN SIZE (land area)... 17th
- STATE SONG... "North Dakota Hymn"
- LARGEST CITY... Fargo

WESTERN MEADOWLARK
WILD PRAIRIE ROSE

STATE SEAL

STATE FLAG

South Dakota

MOUNT RUSHMORE STATE

South Dakota became our 40th state on November 2, 1889. The ★ capital is Pierre. Mt. Rushmore is in South Dakota, as is the prairie that was made famous in the Little House books by Laura Ingalls Wilder. Outlaw Jesse James once escaped capture by jumping a 20-foot chasm at Devil's Gulch. News anchor Tom Brokaw was born and raised in South Dakota.

RING-NECKED
PHEASANT
PASQUE FLOWER

STATE SEAL

STATE FLAG

- CAPITAL... Pierre
- STATE TREE... Black Hills Spruce
- LAND AREA... 75,896 sq. mi.
- RANK IN SIZE (land area)... 16th
- STATE SONG... "Hail South Dakota"
- LARGEST CITY... Sioux Falls

Montana

THE TREASURE STATE

ontana became our 41st state on November 8, 1889. The ★ capital is Helena. Montana is the Spanish word for "mountainous." Antelope, elk, and deer outnumber Montana's two-legged residents. The world's shortest river, the Roe River, runs a whopping 200 feet across the state. A famous landmark is Little Bighorn, where the Sioux and Cheyenne defeated General Custer.

WESTERN
MEADOWLARK
BITTERROOT

STATE SEAL

- CAPITAL... Helena
- STATE TREE... Ponderosa Pine
- LAND AREA... 145,556 sq. mi.
- RANK IN SIZE (land area)... 4th
- STATE SONG... "Montana"
- LARGEST CITY... Billings

STATE FLAG

Washington

THE EVERGREEN STATE

Washington became our 42nd state on November 11, 1889. The ★ capital is Olympia. Washington is named after George Washington and is the only state named after a president.

The first revolving restaurant made its debut in Seattle. More than half the apples eaten in the U.S. are grown in Washington orchards. Washington has more glaciers than all the other "lower 48" states combined.

WILLOW
GOLDFINCH
COAST
RHODODENDRON

STATE SEAL

• CAPITAL... Olympia

• STATE TREE... Western Hemlock

• LAND AREA... 66,581 sq. mi.

• RANK IN SIZE (land area)... 20th

• STATE SONG... "Washington, My Home"

• LARGEST CITY... Seattle

STATE FLAG

Idaho

THE GEM STATE

daho became our 43rd state on July 3, 1890. The ★ capital is Boise. The meaning of the name Idaho is unknown. A U.S. citizen made it up. Idaho is the nation's number one producer of potatoes. The deepest river gorge in North America is Hell's Canyon, deeper than even the Grand Canyon. Television was invented in Idaho in 1926. Idaho is the home state of Olympic Gold Medalist skier Picabo Street.

MOUNTAIN BLUEBIRD
SYRINGA

STATE SEAL

- CAPITAL… Boise
- STATE TREE… Western White Pine
- LAND AREA… 82,751 sq. mi.
- RANK IN SIZE (land area)… 11th
- STATE SONG… "Here We Have Idaho"
- LARGEST CITY… Boise

STATE FLAG

Wyoming

THE EQUALITY STATE

Wyoming became our 44th state on July 10, 1890. The capital is Cheyenne. Wyoming was named by combining two Indian words meaning "at the big flats." This was the first state to give women the right to vote. Yellowstone was the first National Park, and Devil's Tower was the first National Monument. Wyoming is the least populated state in the country.

WESTERN
MEADOWLARK
INDIAN PAINTBRUSH

STATE SEAL

- CAPITAL... Cheyenne
- STATE TREE... Cottonwood
- LAND AREA... 97,105 sq. mi.
- RANK IN SIZE (land area)... 9th
- STATE SONG... "Wyoming"
- LARGEST CITY... Cheyenne

STATE FLAG

Utah

THE BEEHIVE STATE

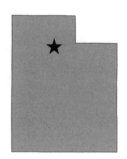

tah became our 45th state on January 4, 1896. The ★ capital is Salt Lake City. Utah comes from an Ute Indian word meaning "people of the mountains." Utah's average peak elevation is the highest in the U.S. The first transcontinental railway was completed in Utah in 1869. Tools dating back 10,000 years have been found in caves in the Utah foothills. Utah's Great Salt Lake, 92 miles long and 48 miles wide, is the largest salt lake in this hemisphere.

AMERICAN SEAGULL
SEGO LILY

STATE SEAL

- CAPITAL... Salt Lake City

- STATE TREE... Blue Spruce

- LAND AREA... 82,168 sq. mi.

- RANK IN SIZE (land area)... 12th

- STATE SONG... "Utah We
                Love Thee"

- LARGEST CITY... Salt Lake City

STATE FLAG

Oklahoma

THE SOONER STATE

SCISSOR-TAILED
FLYCATCHER
MISTLETOE

STATE SEAL

Oklahoma became our 46th state on November 16, 1907. The ★ capital is Oklahoma City. Oklahoma gets its name from Indian words meaning "red person." There are 12 different ecosystems in Oklahoma including mesas, wetlands, sand dunes, and prairies. Two inventions that come from Oklahoma are the shopping cart and the parking meter.

STATE FLAG

- CAPITAL... Oklahoma City
- STATE TREE... Redbud
- LAND AREA... 68,679 sq. mi.
- RANK IN SIZE (land area)... 19th
- STATE SONG... "Oklahoma"
- LARGEST CITY... Oklahoma City

New Mexico

LAND OF ENCHANTMENT

New Mexico became our 47th state on January 6, 1912. The ★ capital is Santa Fe. New Mexico is named from Spanish words meaning "lands north of the Rio Grande." Santa Fe, elevation 7,000 feet, is the highest capital city in the U.S. The world's first atomic bomb was developed in Los Alamos. New Mexico's state flower, the Yucca Plant, can be used for soap and its leaves as a needle and thread. The state bird is the Roadrunner.

- CAPITAL... Santa Fe

- STATE TREE... Piñon Pine

- LAND AREA... 121,365 sq. mi.

- RANK IN SIZE (land area)... 5th

- STATE SONG... "O, Fair New Mexico"

- LARGEST CITY... Albuquerque

ROADRUNNER
YUCCA FLOWER

STATE SEAL

STATE FLAG

Arizona

THE GRAND CANYON STATE

CACTUS WREN
SAGUARO
CACTUS BLOSSOM

STATE SEAL

Arizona became our 48th state on February 14, 1912. The capital is Phoenix. Arizona is the Spanish interpretation of Aztec words meaning "silver bearing." About 550 million years ago, Arizona was under water. As the water receded, it created natural wonders like the Grand Canyon. Today, there are four deserts in Arizona: the Sorrow, Mojave, Great Basin, and Chihuahua.

- CAPITAL... Phoenix

- STATE TREE... Palo Verde

- LAND AREA... 111,642 sq. mi.

- RANK IN SIZE (land area)... 6th

- STATE SONG... "Arizona
                          March Song"

- LARGEST CITY... Phoenix

STATE FLAG

Alaska

THE LAST FRONTIER

Alaska became our 49th state on January 3, 1959. The ★ capital is Juneau. Eskimo words meaning "great lands" give Alaska its name. Alaska has 33,904 square miles of shoreline, more than any other state. Alaska also has more than 100 State Parks and four different climate zones: maritime, arctic, continental, and transitional. During summer in Barrow, Alaska, the sun doesn't set for 84 days.

WILLOW PTARMIGAN   STATE SEAL
FORGET ME NOT

- CAPITAL... Juneau

- STATE TREE... Sitka Spruce

- LAND AREA... 570,374 sq. mi.

- RANK IN SIZE (land area)... 1st

- STATE SONG... "Alaska's Flag"

- LARGEST CITY... Anchorage

STATE FLAG

Hawaii

THE ALOHA STATE

NENE
PUA ALOALO

STATE SEAL

awaii became our 50th state on August 21, 1959. The ★ capital is Honolulu. The name Hawaii is probably based on the Hawaiian word for "volcanic homeland." Hawaii was an island kingdom until Captain Cook claimed it for Britain in 1775. There are only 12 letters in the Hawaiian alphabet. Although Hawaii is not connected to any other state, it somehow manages to have three interstate highways.

- CAPITAL... Honolulu

- STATE TREE... Kukui Candlenut

- LAND AREA... 6,423 sq. mi.

- RANK IN SIZE (land area)... 47th

- STATE SONG... "Hawaii Ponoi"

- LARGEST CITY... Honolulu

STATE FLAG

he United States Mint makes these coins each year: the Lincoln cent; the Jefferson nickel; the Roosevelt dime; the Washington quarter; the Kennedy half dollar; and the Sacagawea dollar. The two larger coins—the half dollar and dollar—are no longer minted for circulation, but you can find older dates at the bank or Post Office. Banks have rolls of these coins, which they will sell to you at face value, although not every bank will have half dollars and dollars.

Collecting coins from pocket change is fun, and a folder or album will help you keep track of which dates you need for your collection.

Lincoln Cents

On August 2, 1909, a cent with a portrait of Abraham Lincoln became America's newest coin. The coin was designed by an artist named Victor David Brenner. A couple years earlier, some of the country's gold coins had been redesigned with the support of President Teddy Roosevelt. He felt that the United States was the greatest nation in the world, and should have the greatest coins. He wanted our coins to be as beautiful as those of ancient Greece.

Theodore Roosevelt (President From 1901 to 1909)
These are some of the coins that were redesigned with Roosevelt's encouragement.

Lincoln Wheat Ears Cent
This is what the Lincoln cent looked like in 1909, when it first came out.

The earliest Lincoln cents had the initials of the engraver, V.D.B., on the reverse. Some people didn't like this, so the initials were removed later that August.

On the back of the coin were two ears of wheat, so people have given it nicknames like "wheat ears penny," "wheat cent," and "wheatie." This design was used from 1909 through 1958.

President Lincoln

In 1918 the V.D.B. initials were put back on the cent, this time in tiny letters on the obverse, on Lincoln's shoulder. In 1943, during World War II, cents were made of steel coated with zinc. This saved copper for the war effort. These steel pennies will stick to a magnet! From 1944 to 1946 cents were made of metal from discarded gun shell cases. In 1947, after the war, the Mint went back to using bronze.

Lincoln Memorial Cent
This is what the one-cent coin looks like today.

In 1959 a new design appeared on the cent, showing the Lincoln Memorial in Washington, DC. The new motif was not very popular (one writer said that it looked like a trolley car!), but it has been used every year since then, for almost 50 years.

Since 1962 the metal used to make cents has changed several times, most recently in 1982. Now the coins are made of zinc plated with copper.

Today, some people think we no longer need a coin as small as the cent. They say that you can't buy anything for a penny anymore. Can you think of anything you can buy for one cent? Do you think the government should get rid of it? Other people want to keep this small coin. They know that the U.S. has made cents every year from 1793 to today, except for one year (1815). It's hard to break that kind of tradition! In the meantime, we have many interesting cents to collect, and you can find most dates and mintmarks in your pocket change.

Indian Head Cent
This is what the one-cent coin looked like before the Lincoln design.

Jefferson Nickels

The obverse of the Jefferson nickel was designed by Felix Schlag, who won an award of $1,000 in a competition with almost 400 other artists. His design was a new direction for the Mint. Earlier nickels and other coins had used symbols, rather than portraits and pictures of real people and places. This one showed President Thomas Jefferson and his home, Monticello.

Five-cent coins were originally made of copper and nickel, which is why people started calling them *nickels*.

Thomas Jefferson (President From 1801 to 1809)

Jefferson Nickel With Monticello
This is what the nickel looked like for more than 65 years.

In 1942, during World War II, a new composition was used for the nickel five-cent coin. Instead of using actual nickel, which was needed for the war effort, the wartime coins used copper, silver, and a metal called manganese. The design was changed, too, to show a large mintmark on the reverse, above Monticello, depending on where each coin was minted: P for Philadelphia, D for Denver, or S for San Francisco. Collectors often call these "war nickels" or "silver nickels." After the war, the Mint started using the old nickel composition again.

The United States Mint began the Westward Journey Nickel Series™ in 2004. The coins in this special program commemorate the bicentennial of the Louisiana Purchase and the journey of Lewis and Clark to explore the vast area recently acquired by the American government.

The 2004 Louisiana Purchase/Peace Medal design was based on the reverse of certain of

Jefferson "Westward Journey" Nickels
There have been many changes on the nickel in recent years.

the original Indian Peace Medals made for the expedition. These medals show a portrait of President Jefferson on one side, and symbols of peace and friendship on the other. They were presented to Native American chiefs and other important leaders as tokens of the goodwill of the United States.

Westward Journey Nickel Holder
There are many ways to display your nickel collection.

The 2004 Keelboat design features an angled side view of the keelboat that carried the Lewis and Clark expedition and their supplies through the rivers of the Louisiana Territory. Built to Captain Lewis's design, this 55-foot keelboat could be sailed, rowed, poled like a raft, or towed from the riverbank.

The 2005 nickels feature a new portrait of President Jefferson. The "Liberty" inscription on the coin is based on his handwriting. The new portrait is inspired by the marble bust of Jefferson completed in 1789 by French sculptor Jean-Antoine Houdon.

The 2005 American Bison design features the familiar "buffalo"—actually a bison. (It resembles the nickel that was made from 1913 to 1938, a popular numismatic design.) Journals from the Lewis and Clark expedition described this large animal, which was very important to many American Indian cultures.

Buffalo Nickel
This is what the nickel looked like before the Jefferson design.

The 2005 "Ocean in View!" design captures the expedition's excitement at finally seeing the Pacific Ocean after many months of arduous travel. It shows a cliffs-and-ocean scene and an inscription inspired by an entry in the journal of Captain William Clark, from November 7, 1805: "Ocean in view! O! The joy!"

In 2006 the nickel features another new portrait of Thomas Jefferson, looking out at the viewer, and an updated view of Monticello.

There are many nice holders and albums for collecting and displaying your Jefferson nickel collection. These coins are fun and easy to collect. You will be able to find many of them in circulation.

Roosevelt Dimes

The United States dime honoring President Franklin D. Roosevelt was designed by Mint Engraver John Sinnock, whose initials, JS, appear at the left of the date.

Roosevelt served as president from 1933 to 1945. During that time he guided the country out of the Great Depression and helped plan the strategy for winning World War II. He died in 1945, a few months before the war ended, while he was still president.

The first Roosevelt dimes came out in January 1946, at the time of the March of Dimes program for that year. The March of Dimes was a campaign started with the president's help in the 1930s, to find a cure for a disease called polio. Roosevelt himself had been crippled by polio in the early 1920s. A doctor named Jonas Salk finally found a cure in 1955.

Roosevelt Dime
This coin was designed shortly after President Roosevelt died.

Roosevelt dimes were made of 90% silver and 10% copper from 1946 through 1964. They were made at all three United States mints. Those struck at Denver and San Francisco had a small D or S at the bottom of the torch. Coins made at the main mint in Philadelphia had no mintmark.

Mintmark Location, 1946–1964
On the reverse, at the bottom of the torch.

Mintmark Location, 1968–Today
On the obverse, above the date.

By 1965, the price of silver was so high that the government had to start using cheaper metal for its coins. Since then, Roosevelt dimes struck for circulation have been made of copper and nickel. However, in 1992 the Mint did start using silver in dimes again, for its Silver Proof sets. Starting in 1968, the mintmark has been on the obverse, above the date.

Roosevelt dimes—both the older silver coins and the modern copper-nickel kind—are inexpensive today and easy to collect. You will be able to find many recent dates in your pocket change. What is the oldest Roosevelt dime you've ever found in change? If you find one from 1964 or before, save it as a "lucky coin"—it's made of real silver!

Mercury Dime
This is what the dime looked like before the Roosevelt design.

Washington Quarters

In 1932 a contest was held to make a new design for the quarter dollar, to honor the 200th anniversary of the birth of George Washington. An artist named John Flanagan won the contest. He made a portrait of Washington based on an old sculpture made in 1785. The reverse showed an eagle standing on a bundle of arrows.

Washington Quarter
When this coin was first made in 1932, George Washington would have been 200 years old.

Bicentennial Quarter
This design shows a colonial drummer and a victory torch surrounded by 13 stars, one for each of the original colonies that started the United States.

Standing Liberty Quarter
This is what the quarter looked like before the Washington design.

Like the Roosevelt dime, circulating Washington quarters were first made in 90% silver and 10% copper. This changed to copper-nickel in 1965. In 1976 a new design celebrated the bicentennial of the Declaration of Independence. Some 40% silver versions of the Bicentennial quarter were struck for special sets.

In 1992 the Mint did start using silver in quarters again, for its Silver Proof sets.

In 1999 the state quarter program was started. Many people have started collecting coins because of the new designs. Which one is your favorite?

Did You Know?
A **bicentennial** is a celebration for a 200-year anniversary.

83

Kennedy Half Dollars

President John F. Kennedy was assassinated on November 22, 1963. The nation was sad to lose this popular president, and people wanted a coin to commemorate his life. A new half dollar was introduced in 1964, showing a portrait of Kennedy and the eagle from the presidential seal. Both of these designs were based on the official presidential Mint medal that was struck when Kennedy became president. The new half dollars were immediately popular not only in the United States but also throughout the world.

The first year, 1964, was the only time Kennedy half dollars were struck in 90% silver for circulation. From 1965 to 1970, 40% silver was used to make them, and then starting in 1971 they've been made in copper-nickel. In 1976 a Bicentennial design honored the 200th anniversary of the Declaration of Independence—the birth of the nation. Some 40% silver versions of the Bicentennial half dollar were struck for special sets. In recent years the half dollar has been struck only for the Mint's Proof and Mint sets, and not for circulation. However, in 1992 the Mint did start using silver again, for its Silver Proof sets.

Kennedy Half Dollar
This coin was designed to honor President John F. Kennedy, who was killed in 1963.

Bicentennial Half Dollar
The 1776–1976 design shows Independence Hall in Philadelphia.

Benjamin Franklin Half Dollar
This is what the half dollar looked like before the Kennedy design.

The Kennedy half dollar is a neat, big coin with a lot of history. You probably won't find many in pocket change, but you can go to the bank and ask if they have any rolls of half dollars. If they do, you can buy them for face value—40 coins at 50¢ apiece, or $20 per roll. Save the ones you need for your collection, and then take the rest back to the bank or spend them! Sometimes people find old silver half dollars in bank rolls. Who knows… maybe you'll be lucky and find some, too.

Sacagawea Dollars

Congress passed the United States Dollar Coin Act in 1997. This authorized a new dollar coin that would be gold in color, 26.5 mm wide, and have an edge that was different from other coins. The Secretary of the Treasury had some design rules for the new dollar:

1. the obverse must show one or more women,
2. it could not show a living person, and
3. the reverse must show an eagle.

The obverse shows Sacagawea, a Shoshone Indian girl who helped guide Lewis and Clark as they explored America's western lands in the early 1800s. She is shown with her baby son, Jean Baptiste, whose nickname was Pomp.

Sacagawea Dollar
Stamp machines at the Post Office will often give this coin as change.

Without Sacagawea, the expedition might have failed. She helped Lewis and Clark get horses for the journey, and taught them how to find plants that were safe to eat. When other Native Americans encountered the group and saw a young woman and child with them, they knew that Lewis and Clark were not looking for war, but were on a peaceful mission. With her encouragement, the Native Americans gave help when Lewis and Clark needed it. Sacagawea even saved some of Captain Clark's

Susan B. Anthony Dollar
This earlier dollar coin also showed a woman: civil rights pioneer Susan B. Anthony.

diaries and other important materials when their boat turned over in the Missouri River.

The reason the United States Dollar Coin Act said the coin's edge had to be different was because in the 1970s and '80s, some people got confused and thought the Susan B. Anthony dollar was actually a quarter. It was about the size of a quarter, and the same color as a quarter, and both coins had *reeded* edges (with lines going up and down around the edge). The Sacagawea dollar has a smooth edge.

This coin is sometimes called the "Golden Dollar," but it doesn't really have any gold in it. The coin is made mostly of copper and zinc, with a little nickel and manganese. These metals combine to make a golden color. With its smooth edge and unique color, nobody will mistake the Sacagawea dollar for a quarter!

*O*nce you start collecting and learning about coins, you might think about joining a coin club, association, or society. There are many such groups throughout the United States and Canada. Some of them are local clubs that meet one or twice a month, hold coin shows and auctions, and put on presentations for and by members. Others are larger national groups that communicate mainly through newsletters, email, and once-a-year meetings. And some are national or international clubs with thousands of members and smaller, state-based chapters.

Many of these groups welcome young collectors and even have special "Young Numismatist" meetings and activities. Older members know that new collectors are the future of the hobby, and they enjoy sharing their knowledge and experience.

Look in your local phone book or ask a nearby coin shop owner if there are any local or regional groups in your city. Also, here are some national groups you might be interested in. There are many more to consider, so ask around and see if there's one perfect for you!

American Numismatic Association. www.money.org. One of the largest numismatic organizations in the world, the ANA has more than 30,000 members. It promotes studying and collecting money for research, interpretation, and preservation of history and culture from ancient times to the present.

Canadian Numismatic Association. www.canadian-numismatic.org. Many United States collectors also collect coins of our neighbor to the north. The CNA promotes fellowship, communication, and education, and provides advocacy and leadership for the hobby.

Civil War Token Society. www.cwtsociety.com. The CWTS is a national, non-profit organization that stimulates interest and research in the field of Civil War token collecting. It publishes the *Civil War Token Journal*, conducts auctions, maintains a reference library, provides an attribution service, establishes state chapters, and conducts regional meetings.

Colonial Coin Collectors Club. www.colonialcoins.org. This club provides a forum for collectors of numismatic material related to the Early American era—coins, tokens, currency, and medals.

CONECA. www.conecaonline.org. This national organization is devoted to the education of error and variety coin collectors. CONECA focuses on many error and variety specialties—doubled dies, repunched mintmarks, double strikes, off-centered coin, etc.

Early America Coppers. www.eacs.org. EAC serves as a point of contact for collectors of early U.S. copper coins—colonials, half cents, large cents, and Hard Time tokens. Its bi-monthly magazine, *Penny-Wise*, contains numerous original articles pertaining to early coppers.

Numismatic Bibliomania Society. www.coinbooks.org. The NBS supports and promotes the use and collecting of numismatic literature—books, periodicals, catalogs and other written or printed material relating to coins, medals, tokens, or paper money, ancient or modern, U.S. or worldwide.

Society of Paper Money Collectors. www.spmc.org. The SPMC is open to anyone interested in paper money or related areas such as checks, stocks, engravings, and other fiscal ephemera (items that had only temporary value, such as circus tickets).

Token and Medal Society. www.tokenandmedal.org. This educational society promotes the study and collecting of exonumia, consisting of tokens, medals, badges and other related items.

Connect the Collectibles!

Connect the coin or other collectible with the people who study it.

American Numismatic Association

Canadian Numismatic Association

Civil War Token Society

Colonial Coin Collectors Club

CONECA

Early American Coppers

Numismatic Bibliomania Society

Society of Paper Money Collectors

Token and Medal Society

*T*hese books will give you more information on United States coins you can collect. You will learn about their history, rarity, values, and other interesting facts. These are just a few of the books people have written about coins!

COLONIAL ISSUES

Breen, Walter. *Walter Breen's Complete Encyclopedia of U.S. and Colonial Coins*, New York, 1988.

Crosby, S. S. *The Early Coins of America*, Boston, 1875 (reprinted 1945, 1965, 1974, 1983).

Newman, Eric P., and Doty, Richard G. *Studies on Money in Early America*, New York, 1976.

Rulau, Russell, and Fuld, George. *Medallic Portraits of Washington*, Iola, WI, 1999.

HISTORY OF THE U.S. MINT

Lange, David W. *History of the United States Mint and Its Coinage*, Atlanta, GA, 2005.

HALF CENTS

Breen, Walter. *Walter Breen's Encyclopedia of United States Half Cents 1793–1857*, South Gate, CA, 1983.

Cohen, Roger S., Jr. *American Half Cents—The "Little Half Sisters"* (2nd ed.), 1982.

LARGE CENTS

Breen, Walter. *Walter Breen's Encyclopedia of Early United States Cents 1793–1814*, Wolfeboro, NH, 2001.

Newcomb, H.R. *United States Copper Cents 1816–1857*, New York, 1944 (reprinted 1983).

PENNY-WISE, official publication of Early American Coppers, Inc.

Sheldon, William H. *Penny Whimsy (1793–1814)*, New York, 1958 (reprinted 1965, 1976).

SMALL CENTS

Fivaz, Bill, and Stanton, J.T. *The Cherrypickers' Guide to Rare Die Varieties*, Savannah, GA, 1994.

Lange, David W. *The Complete Guide to Lincoln Cents*, Wolfeboro, NH, 1996.

Wexler, John, and Flynn, Kevin. *The Authoritative Reference on Lincoln Cents*, Rancocas, NJ, 1996.

TWO-CENT PIECES

Flynn, Kevin. *Getting Your Two Cents Worth*, Rancocas, NJ, 1994.

Kliman, Myron M. *The Two Cent Piece and Varieties*, South Laguna, CA, 1977.

NICKEL FIVE-CENT PIECES

Bowers, Q. David. *A Guide Book of Shield and Liberty Head Nickels*, Atlanta, GA, 2006.

Bowers, Q. David. *A Guide Book of Buffalo and Jefferson Nickels*, Atlanta, GA, 2006.

Wescott, Michael. *The United States Nickel Five-Cent Piece*, Wolfeboro, NH, 1991.

HALF DIMES

Blythe, Al. *The Complete Guide to Liberty Seated Half Dimes*, Virginia Beach, VA, 1992.

Logan, Russell, and McClosky, John. *Federal Half Dimes 1792–1837*, Manchester, MI, 1998.

DIMES

Flynn, Kevin. *The Authoritative Reference on Roosevelt Dimes*, Brooklyn, NY, 2001.

Greer, Brian. *The Complete Guide to Liberty Seated Dimes*, Virginia Beach, VA, 1992.

Kosoff, A. *United States Dimes From 1796*, New York, 1945.

Lange, David W. *The Complete Guide to Mercury Dimes*, Virginia Beach, VA 1993.

Lawrence, David. *The Complete Guide to Barber Dimes*, Virginia Beach, VA 1991.

QUARTER DOLLARS

Bressett, Kenneth. *The Official Whitman Statehood Quarters Collector's Handbook*, New York, 2000.

Cline, J.H. *Standing Liberty Quarters* (3rd ed.), 1996.

Duphorne, R. *The Early Quarter Dollars of the United States*, 1975.

Lawrence, David. *The Complete Guide to Barber Quarters*, Virginia Beach, VA, 1989.

HALF DOLLARS

Fox, Bruce. *The Complete Guide to Walking Liberty Half Dollars*, Virginia Beach, VA, 1993.

Lawrence, David. *The Complete Guide to Barber Halves*, Virginia Beach, VA, 1991.

Overton, Al C. *Early Half Dollar Die Varieties 1794-1836*, Colorado Springs, CO, 1967 (3rd ed., 1990, edited by Donald Parsley).

Wiley, Randy, and Bugert, Bill. *The Complete Guide to Liberty Seated Half Dollars*, Virginia Beach, VA, 1993.

SILVER DOLLARS

Bowers, Q. David. *Silver Dollars and Trade Dollars of the United States: A Complete Encyclopedia*, Wolfeboro, NH, 1993.

Bowers, Q. David. *A Guide Book of Morgan Silver Dollars: A Complete History and Price Guide* (2nd ed.), Atlanta, GA, 2005.

Newman, Eric P., and Bressett, Kenneth E. *The Fantastic 1804 Dollar*, Racine, WI, 1962.

GOLD PIECES ($1 THROUGH $20)

Akers, David W. *Gold Dollars (and Other Gold Denominations)*, Englewood, OH, 1975–1982.

Bowers, Q. David. *A Guide Book of Double Eagle Gold Coins*, Atlanta, GA, 2004.

Bowers, Q. David. *United States Gold Coins: An Illustrated History*, Wolfeboro, NH, 1982.

COMMEMORATIVES

Bowers, Q. David. *Commemorative Coins of the United States: A Complete Encyclopedia*, Wolfeboro, NH, 1991.

Swiatek, Anthony, and Breen, Walter. *The Encyclopedia of United States Silver and Gold Commemorative Coins 1892–1954*, New York, 1981.

TOKENS

Rulau, Russell. *Standard Catalog of United States Tokens 1700–1900*, Iola, WI, 1997.

Fuld, George, and Fuld, Melvin. *U.S. Civil War Store Cards*, Lawrence, MA, 1975.

PATTERNS

Judd, J. Hewitt. *United States Pattern Coins* (9th ed., edited by Q. David Bowers), Atlanta, GA, 2005.

PROOF COINS AND PROOF SETS

Lange, David W. *A Guide Book of Modern United States Proof Coin Sets*, Atlanta, GA, 2005.

TYPE COINS

Bowers, Q. David. *A Guide Book of United States Type Coins*, Atlanta, GA, 2005.

Garrett, Jeff, and Guth, Ron. *100 Greatest U.S. Coins* (2nd ed.), Atlanta, GA, 2005.

Guth, Ron, and Garrett, Jeff. *United States Coinage: A Study by Type*, Atlanta, GA, 2005.

O ver the years coin collectors have developed a special jargon to describe their coins. The following list includes terms that are used frequently by coin collectors or that have a special meaning other than their ordinary dictionary definitions. You will find them useful when you want to discuss or describe your coins.

A

alloy—A combination of two or more metals.

altered date—A false date on a coin; a date altered to make a coin appear to be one of a rarer or more valuable issue.

B

bag mark—A surface mark, usually a small nick, acquired by a coin through contact with others in a mint bag.

billon—A low-grade alloy of silver (usually less than 50%) mixed with another metal, typically copper.

blank—The formed piece of metal on which a coin design will be stamped.

bronze—An alloy of copper, zinc, and tin.

bullion—Uncoined gold or silver in the form of bars, ingots, or plate.

business strike—An Uncirculated coin intended for eventual use in commerce, as opposed to a Proof coin.

C

cast coins—Coins that are made by pouring molten metal into a mold, instead of in the usual manner of striking with dies.

cent—One one-hundredth of the standard monetary unit. Also known as a *centavo*, *centimo*, or *centesimo* in some Central American and South American countries; *centime* in France and various former colonies in Africa; and other variations.

certified coin—A coin that has been graded, authenticated, and encapsulated in plastic by an independent grading service.

cherrypicker—A collector who finds scarce and unusual coins by carefully searching through old accumulations or dealers' stocks.

clad coinage—Issues of the United States dimes, quarters, halves, and dollars made since 1965. Each coin has a center core of pure copper and a layer of copper–nickel or silver on both sides.

collar—The outer ring, or die chamber, that holds a blank in place in the coinage press while the coin is impressed with the obverse and reverse dies.

contact marks—Minor abrasions on an uncirculated coin, made by contact with other coins in a bag or roll.

countermark—A stamp or mark impressed on a coin to verify its use by another government or to indicate revaluation.

crack-out—A coin that has been removed from an encapsulated grading service holder.

crown—Any dollar-size coin (c. 38 mm in diameter) in general, often struck in silver; specifically, one from the United Kingdom and some Commonwealth countries.

D

designer—The artist who creates a coin's design. An engraver is the person who cuts a design into a coinage die.

die—A piece of metal engraved with a design and used for stamping coins.

die crack—A fine, raised line on a coin, caused by a broken die.

die defect—An imperfection on a coin, caused by a damaged die.

die variety—Any minor alteration in the basic design of a coin.

dipped, dipping—Refers to chemical cleaning of a coin with diluted acid.

double eagle—The United States $20 gold coin.

doubled die—A die that that been given two misaligned impressions from a hub; also, a coin made from such a die.

doubloon—Popular name for a Spanish gold coin originally valued at $16.00.

eagle—A United States $10 gold coin; also refers to U.S. silver, gold, and platinum bullion pieces made from 1986 to the present.

E

edge—Periphery of a coin, often containing a series of reeds, lettering, or other decoration.

electrotype—A reproduction of a coin or medal made by the electrodeposition process. Electrotypes are frequently used in museum displays.

electrum—A naturally occurring mixture of gold and silver. Some of the world's first coins were made of this alloy.

encapsulated coins—Coins that have been authenticated, graded, and sealed in plastic by a professional service.

engraver—The person who cuts the design into a coinage die.

error—A mismade coin not intended for circulation.

exergue—That portion of a coin beneath the main design, often separated from it by a line, and typically bearing the date.

F

field—The background portion of a coin's surface not used for a design or inscription.

filler—A coin in worn condition but rare enough to be included in a collection.

fineness—The purity of gold, silver, or any other precious metal, expressed in terms of one thousand parts. A coin of 90% pure silver is expressed as .900 fine.

flan—A blank piece of metal in the size and shape of a coin; also called a planchet.

G

gem—A coin of exceptionally high quality.

H

half eagle—The United States $5 gold coin minted from 1795 to 1929.

hub—A positive-image punch to impress the coin's design into a die for coinage.

I

incuse—The design of a coin which has been impressed below the coin's surface. A design raised above the coin's surface is in relief.

inscription—The legend or lettering on a coin.

intrinsic value—Bullion or "melt" value of the actual precious metal in a numismatic item.

investment grade—Generally, a coin in grade MS-65 or better.

J

junk silver—Common-date silver coins taken from circulation; worth only bullion value.

K

key coin—The scarcest or most valuable coin in a series.

L

laureate—Head crowned with a laurel wreath.

legal tender—Money that is officially issued and recognized for redemption by an authorized agency or government.

legend—The principal inscription on a coin.

lettered edge—The narrow edge of a coin bearing an inscription, found on some foreign and most older United States coins.

luster—The brilliant or "frosty" surface quality of an Uncirculated (Mint State) coin.

M

milled edge—The raised rim around the outer surface of a coin, not to be confused with the reeded or serrated narrow edge of a coin.

mint error—Any mismade or defective coin produced by a mint.

mint luster—Shiny "frost" or brilliance on the surface of an Uncirculated or Mint State coin.

mintmark—A small letter on a coin, indicating the mint at which it was struck.

Mint set—A set of Uncirculated coins packaged and sold by the Mint. Each set contains one of each of the coins made for circulation at each of the mints.

motto—An inspirational word or phrase used on a coin.

mule—A coin struck from two dies not originally intended to be used together.

O

obverse—The front or face side of a coin.

overdate—Date made by superimposing one or more numerals on a previously dated die.

over graded—A coin in poorer condition than stated.

overstrike—An impression made with new dies on a previously struck coin.

P

patina—The green or brown surface film found on ancient copper and bronze coins, caused by oxidation over a long period of time.

pattern—Experimental or trial coin, generally of a new design, denomination, or metal.

pedigree—The record of previous owners of a rare coin.

planchet—The blank piece of metal on which a coin design is stamped.

Proofs—Coins struck for collectors by the Mint using specially polished dies and planchets.

Proof set—A set of each of the Proof coins made during a given year, packaged by the Mint and sold to collectors.

Q

quarter eagle—The United States $2.50 gold coin.

R

raw — A coin that has not been encapsulated by an independent grading service.

reeded edge — The edge of a coin with grooved lines that run vertically around its perimeter, as seen on modern United States silver and clad coins.

relief — Any part of a coin's design that is raised above the coin's field is said to be in relief. The opposite of relief is incuse, meaning sunk into the field.

restrike — A coin struck from genuine dies at a later date than the original issue.

reverse — The back side of a coin.

rim — The raised portion of a coin that protects the design from wear.

round — A round one-ounce silver medal or bullion piece.

S

series — A set of one coin of each year of a specific design and denomination issued from each mint. For example, Lincoln cents from 1909 to 1959.

slab — A hard plastic case containing a coin that has been graded and encapsulated by a professional service.

spot price — The daily quoted market value of precious metals in bullion form.

T

token — A privately issued piece, typically with an exchange value for goods or services, but not an official government coin.

trade dollar — Silver dollar issued especially for trade with a foreign country. In the United States, Trade dollars were first issued in 1873 to stimulate commerce with the Orient. Many other countries have also issued trade dollars.

truncation — The sharply cut-off bottom edge of a bust or portrait.

type — A series of coins defined by a shared distinguishing design, composition, denomination, and other elements. For example, Barber dimes or Franklin half dollars.

type set — A collection consisting of one representative coin of each type, of a particular series or period.

U

Uncirculated — A business strike coin that has never been used in commerce, and has retained its original surface and luster; also called Mint State.

unique — An item of which only one specimen is known to exist.

variety — A coin's design that sets it apart from the normal issue of that type.

W

wheaties — Lincoln cents with the wheat ears reverse, issued from 1909 to 1958.

Y

year set — A set of coins for any given year, consisting of one of each denomination issued that year.